D0820826

Patternmaking in Fashion Step by Step

La création des patrons de mode pas à pas

Schnittmuster entwerfen Schritt für Schritt

Patternmaking in Fashion Step by Step

La création des patrons de mode pas à pas

Schnittmuster entwerfen Schritt für Schritt

evergreen

© 2010 EVERGREEN GmbH, Köln

Editorial coordination: Anja Llorella Oriol

Editor, texts and illustrations: Lucia Mors de Castro

Photography: Inka Recke

Model: Agnes Armah

Digital illustrations: Guillermo Pfaff Puigmartí

Text editing: Anja Llorella Oriol

Translations and proof-reading: Cillero & de Motta

Art Director: Emma Termes Parera

Graphic design and layout: Maira Purman

Printed in Spain

ISBN 978-3-8365-1721-8

Cut by cut
A book about dressmaking

The earliest documents on dressmaking date back to the 16th century. These were really plans designed to facilitate the cutting process and waste the least amount of fabric possible. In those days, using a pattern adapted to fit the figure was frowned upon since a good tailor could transfer the body measurements straight on to the cloth and adjust its form on the client to achieve a perfect fit. Each order was completed separately, and if the same client placed a new order, the whole process was started from scratch again. This gave rise to exclusive models made to measure.

By the 19th century, women's magazines came with dressmaking patterns. Decorative motifs and fabric samples became less significant, with greater importance being attached to the shape and how it was made to fit the body.

With the invention of the sewing machine, increasing industrialization, and with it the start of mass production, it became necessary to use standardized clothing sizes, which were created by taking the measurements of large sectors of the population. This led to the unlimited reproduction of successful models, which completely revolutionized the fashion world. As a result, customers today can choose from an almost unlimited range of styles, materials, and colors.

When we choose a particular model from the wide variety of options available to us because we think it is the one that best reflects our taste, there is a strong likelihood that it will have been largely influenced by what is currently in vogue at the time. If, despite the huge selection available, we decide to make our own clothes, the main reason may be because we want to feel as comfortable as possible. Furthermore, this option enables us to reflect our own

Coupe par coupe
Un livre sur la coupe et la confection

Les premiers documents sur la coupe et la confection remontent au XVIème siècle. Il s'agissait plutôt de plans destinés à faciliter la coupe afin de perdre le moins de tissu possible. À cette époque, l'utilisation d'un patron adapté à la mesure du corps était désapprouvée, étant donné qu'un bon tailleur pouvait transposer les mesures du corps directement sur le tissu et modeler parfaitement la forme sur le client. Chaque commande était réalisée séparément et si un même client en passait une nouvelle, on recommençait à zéro. C'est ainsi que sont apparus les modèles uniques coupés sur mesure.

Au XIXème siècle, les revues pour femmes incluent des patrons. La valeur de la décoration et la conception des tissus étaient de moins en moins importantes, à l'inverse de la forme et l'adaptation au corps.

Avec l'invention de la machine à coudre, l'industrialisation toujours croissante et, de ce fait, le début de la production à grande échelle, il est devenu indispensable d'utiliser des tailles standardisées de confection, qui ont été créées en prenant les mesures de grands groupes de population. C'est ainsi qu'a été obtenue la reproduction illimitée d'un modèle à succès, ce qui a totalement révolutionné le monde de la mode. C'est grâce à cela que les clients d'aujourd'hui peuvent choisir parmi une offre presque illimitée de style, matériaux et couleurs.

Lorsque nous sélectionnons un certain modèle parmi la grande variété d'options disponibles, parce que nous croyons que c'est le mieux adapté à nos goûts, il y a de grandes chances que ceux-ci aient été influencés en grande mesure par la mode régnant à ce moment. Malgré l'offre impressionnante, si nous décidons de coudre nous-mêmes nos vêtements, il est possible que ce soit surtout pour

Schnitt für Schnitt
Ein Buch über Schnitt

Die frühesten erhaltenen Schnittdokumente stammen aus dem 16. Jahrhundert. Es sind eher Auflagepläne, die den Zuschnitt mit möglichst wenig Verschnitt erleichtern sollten. Die Verwendung eines Schnittes nach Körpermaßen war damals noch verpönt, denn ein guter Schneider konnte die am Körper gemessenen Maße direkt auf den Stoff übertragen und die perfekte Form dann am Kunden modellieren. Jeder Auftrag wurde so einzeln bearbeitet und im Falle einer Folgebestellung immer wieder von vorne begonnen. Es entstanden maßgeschneiderte Unikate.

Aus dem 19. Jahrhundert sind Schnitte aus „Frauen-Magazinen" erhalten. Dekorationen und Stoffmustern wurde immer weniger, der Passform dagegen immer größerer Wert beigemessen.

Mit der Erfindung der Nähmaschine, der immer stärkeren Industrialisierung und dem damit einhergehenden Beginn der Massenproduktion wurde die Verwendung von standardisierten Konfektionsgrößen unabdingbar, die durch das Vermessen ganzer Bevölkerungsgruppen ermittelt wurden; so ließ sich die unbegrenzte Reproduktion eines erfolgreichen Modells erreichen, was den Modebereich vollkommen revolutionierte. Wie selbstverständlich können heute die Käufer aus einem scheinbar unbegrenzten Angebot an Stilen, Materialien und Farben auswählen.

Wenn aus der angebotenen Modellvielfalt die Wahl auf ein ganz bestimmtes fällt, weil es scheinbar dem eigenen Geschmack entspricht, dann ist die Wahrscheinlichkeit, dass dieser vermutlich bereits von der gerade vorherrschenden Mode stark beeinflusst ist, recht groß. Entscheidet man sich trotz des enormen Angebots dafür, sich die Kleidung selbst auf den Leib zu schneidern, so dürfte der Hauptgrund darin liegen, sich in ihr so wohl wie möglich zu

ideas and concepts, and the satisfaction perceived with our own creative efforts and "doing it ourselves" endows the character of a garment with an even greater value.

To create fashion nothing more than paper, pencil, ruler and a table are required, in addition to ideas, curiosity, ambition, concentration and endurance. In the following pages we shall present all the current techniques, formulas and tricks of the trade to create a garment that is a perfect fit. Taking basic patterns as our starting point, we shall begin by developing creative models, fostering an understanding and sensitivity of the body's dimensions and revealing the logical, geometric rules of artistic modeling. The variations of models shown here are described in full and are based on basic patterns. However, only a fraction of the varied and unlimited number of creative possibilities can be included here. Nevertheless a large number of common learning concepts and details are provided, and, if developed, these can be applied to whatever idea for design you have in mind.

By addressing these basic concepts, one soon becomes aware of the thought and work processes that lie behind a finished garment. Furthermore, this book also seeks to convey part of the fascination that ensues from developing and creating garments, working with paper and cloth, and the varied language of shapes in the world of fashion.

nous sentir le plus confortable possible. En outre, nous pouvons représenter nos idées et conceptions dans la réalité et la satisfaction ressentie de notre propre créativité et par « ce fait main » confèrent encore plus de valeur au caractère d'un vêtement.

Pour créer de la mode, il faut juste du papier, un crayon, une règle et une table, outre des idées, de la curiosité, de l'ambition, de la concentration et de la persévérance. Dans les pages suivantes, nous allons vous présenter les techniques, formules et astuces actuelles pour obtenir un vêtement adapté individuellement à notre corps. En partant des patrons de base, nous parlerons du développement de modèles créatifs, stimulerons la compréhension et la sensibilité aux dimensions du corps et révélerons les règles logiques et géométriques du modelage plastique. Tous les modèles présentés ici sont décrits en détail et s'appuient sur des patrons de base mais il est seulement possible de montrer une faible part des possibilités de création variées et illimitées. Cependant, ils incluent un grand nombre de concepts d'apprentissage habituels et des détails qui, s'ils sont développés, peuvent s'appliquer à n'importe quelle idée de design souhaitée.

Le fait d'aborder ces concepts de base permet de comprendre rapidement le processus de pensée et de travail qui se dissimule derrière un vêtement terminé. De plus, ce livre a pour finalité de transmettre une partie de la fascination que suscite le développement de vêtements, le travail avec du papier et des tissus et le langage varié des formes dans le cadre de la mode.

fühlen. Darüber hinaus lassen sich eigene Ideen und Vorstellungen realisieren, und die Zufriedenheit, die aus dem kreativen, anpackenden „Selber-tun" entsteht, wertet den Charakter eines Kleidungsstückes noch zusätzlich auf.

Um Mode zu entwerfen, braucht man eigentlich nicht mehr als Papier, einen Stift, Lineale und einen Tisch; daneben Ideen, Neugier, Ehrgeiz, Konzentration und Durchhaltevermögen. Auf den folgenden Seiten werden alle wesentlichen Techniken, Formeln und Kniffe vorgestellt, um dem Körper eine individuell passende Hülle zu schaffen. Ausgehend von den Grundschnitten, wird in die kreative Modellentwicklung eingeführt, indem Verständnis und Gefühl für die Dimensionen des Körpers geweckt und die logischen, geometrischen Regeln der plastischen Formenarbeit aufgezeigt werden. Die hier abgebildeten, ausführlich beschriebenen und auf den Grundschnitten basierenden Modellvariationen können natürlich nur einen kleinen Teil der vielfältigen und unbegrenzten Möglichkeiten an Kreationen demonstrieren. Sie enthalten allerdings eine große Zahl typischer Lernschritte und Details, die weiter entwickelt, für jede beliebige Designidee angewendet werden können.

In der Auseinandersetzung mit diesen Grundkonzepten stellt sich schon bald ein gewisses Bewusstsein für den Gedanken- und Arbeitsprozess ein, der hinter einem fertigen Kleidungsstück steht. Darüber hinaus soll dieses Buch etwas von der Faszination vermitteln, die das Entwerfen und Fertigen von Kleidung, die Arbeit mit Papier und Stoff und die vielfältige Formensprache der Mode wecken.

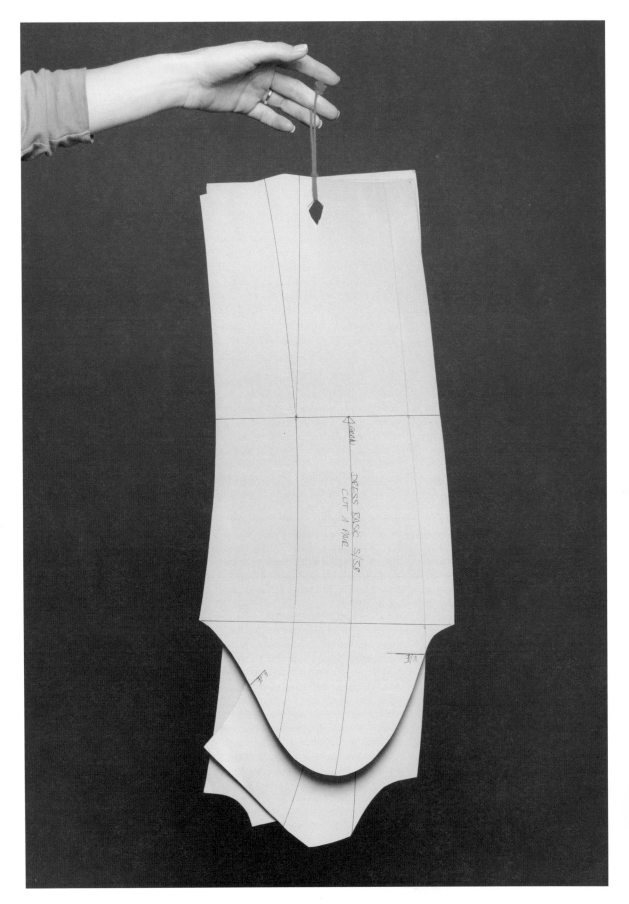

Developing patterns

1. A pattern is what we call the paper or cardboard template used to cut out the fabric. Each part of a garment, such as the front and back, pockets, collar, sleeves or pant legs, needs its own pattern piece. This pattern can be created from the measurements of an individual person, or on an industrial scale using the measurements of a standard size.

Pattern designing is based on theoretical considerations and calculations. It is not about vague suggestions, but logical solutions reflected on paper. A pattern is a technical introduction, responding to certain reasons, inviting us to get down to work, and, in its simple form on paper, represents an entire design project. It guarantees the achievement of a model, either as a one-off or for mass production.

There are various pattern systems, and they all have their advantages and disadvantages. Typically they all use a certain order, formulas and modules, which can be applied according to the measurements taken to obtain a reliable result. Thus, it is important to understand the technique right from the beginning so as to gain a solid basis on which to start developing and experimenting. The methods shown here do not correspond to any specific system for designing patterns but are based on the knowledge of the system developed by Müller & Sohn München, which can be extended through tests, experiments and exchanges with other colleagues and pattern systems.

The challenge of designing patterns lies in being able to create a basis for a three-dimensional garment on a two-dimensional surface. The pattern specifies both the size of the surface and the dimension for the depth. The paper pattern often takes on forms that are difficult to understand because of their curves and projections, and the design cannot be appreciated until the

Le développement de patrons

1. Nous appelons patron le modèle en papier ou carton utilisé pour couper le tissu. Chaque partie d'un vêtement comme, par exemple, le devant et le dos, les poches, le cou, les manches ou les jambes, nécessite sa propre pièce de patron. Ce patron peut être créé à partir des mesures d'une personne ou à l'échelle industrielle, selon la mesure d'une taille standard.

La fabrication de patrons repose sur des réflexions théoriques et de calcul. Il ne s'agit pas de suggestions imprécises mais de solutions logiques représentées sur du papier. Un patron est une introduction technique, il correspond à des raisons, il nous invite à nous mettre au travail et implique, dans sa forme simple en papier, tout un plan de conception. Il garantit l'obtention d'un modèle, aussi bien d'une pièce unique que d'une production industrielle.

Il existe plusieurs systèmes de patrons et tous ont des avantages et de inconvénients. Ils ont comme caractéristique commune de tous utiliser un certain ordre, des formules et des modules, qui peuvent s'appliquer selon les mesures prises pour obtenir un résultat fiable. Pour ce faire, il est important de comprendre la technique depuis le début, pour disposer d'une base solide sur laquelle commencer à développer et expérimenter. Les pratiques présentées ici ne correspondent à aucun système complet de patronage mais se basent sur les connaissances du système Müller & Sohn München et peuvent être améliorées par des essais, des expériences et un échange avec d'autres collègues et systèmes de patronage.

Le défi de la conception de patrons consiste à créer la base d'un vêtement tridimensionnel sur une surface bidimensionnelle. Le patron précise la taille de la surface, ainsi que la dimension de profondeur. Il

Die Schnittenwicklung

1. Als Schnitt bezeichnet man die Papier- oder Kartonschablonen, nach denen der Stoff zugeschnitten wird. Für jedes Teil eines Kleidungsstücks, wie beispielsweise Vorder- und Rückenteil, Taschen, Kragen, Ärmel und Passen, gibt es das entsprechende Schnittteil. Dieser Schnitt kann in Maßarbeit für eine individuelle Person erstellt werden oder auch industriell entsprechend der Maße einer ermittelten Standardgröße.

Schnittarbeit beruht auf theoretischen und rechnerischen Überlegungen; es handelt sich nicht um vage Vorschläge, sondern logische Lösungen, die auf dem Papier entstehen. Ein Schnitt ist eine technische Anleitung, verspricht Handhabe, lädt zum Tun ein und beinhaltet in seiner starren Papierform den Plan des Designs. Er gewährleistet die Fertigung eines Modells, sei es als Einzelstück oder in industrieller Produktion.

Es existieren diverse Schnittsysteme nebeneinander, die alle sowohl Vor- als auch Nachteile aufweisen. Gemein ist allen, dass sie gewisse Reihenfolgen, Formeln und Module benutzen, die auf die jeweilig gemessenen Maße angewendet werden können und so zu einem zuverlässigen Ergebnis führen. Daher ist es wichtig, die Technik von Grund auf zu verstehen, um so eine solide Basis zu besitzen, auf die man sich beim Entwerfen und Experimentieren stützen kann. Die hier vorgestellten Übungen folgen keinem konkreten Schnittsystem, basieren jedoch auf den Erkenntnissen mit dem System Müller & Sohn München, das durch Ausprobieren, Erfahrungen und im Austausch mit Kollegen und anderen Schnittsystemen erweitert wurde.

Die besondere Herausforderung des Schnittzeichnens besteht darin, auf einer zweidimensionalen Fläche die Anleitung für ein dreidimensionales Kleidungsstück

  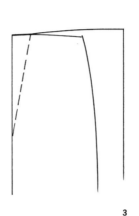 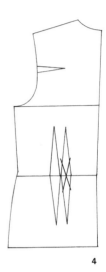

1   2   3   4

pattern is transferred to the fabric, the individual pieces are sewn up and the darts added.

1-2-3-4. Darts are tucks in the form of a triangle that end at a point and are used in non-stretch fabrics. They occupy a fixed position in the preparation of the basic pattern. Necessary adjustments are best made in the darts when fitting the garment. On the other hand, when making up the pattern, their position is often unclear. "They disappear" between the seams, they are traced on the paper pattern in such a way that it is not clear what they are, or else they look like some kind of decorative item.

If we wish to move a dart, we should bear in mind that it fits the contours of the body best in its original position. For this reason, a dart should only be moved to a parallel position, as shown in the example of the waistline dart in the illustration, and only as far as is absolutely necessary.

We recommend never moving a dart more than 3-4 centimeters.

5-6. Another way to alter the position of the darts is to transfer them. First of all, decide where to move the dart and trace it on the paper in its new position. The original dart

arrive souvent que le patron en papier ait des formes difficiles à comprendre du fait de ses courbes et saillies et que la représentation plastique n'apparaisse pas avant de le transférer au tissu, de coudre les pièces individuelles et de commencer à utiliser les pinces.

1-2-3-4. Les pinces sont des plis en forme de coins terminant en pointe et utilisés dans des tissus non élastiques. Elles occupent une position fixe dans la confection du patron de base. C'est pendant l'essai qu'il vaut mieux apporter les corrections nécessaires aux pinces. Par contre, lors de la construction du patron, leur position est souvent erronée. Elles « disparaissent » entre les coutures, se dessinent sur le patron en papier de telle manière que l'on ne sait pas ce que c'est ou ressemblent à un élément décoratif.

Si nous voulons déplacer une pince, nous devons tenir compte du fait que c'est dans sa position originale qu'elle s'adaptait le mieux à la forme du corps. Pour ce faire, une pince doit uniquement être déplacée parallèlement comme, par exemple, la pince de la taille de l'image, sur la juste distance nécessaire. Il est recommandé que ce déplacement ne soit jamais supérieur à 3-4 centimètres.

zu erarbeiten. Das Schnittmuster gibt sowohl die Oberflächenexpansion also auch die Tiefendimension des Modells an. Oft nimmt der Papierschnitt durch seine Aus- und Einbuchtungen schwer nachvollziehbare Formen an, und erst durch deren Übertragung auf den Stoff und das Verbinden der einzelnen Teile durch Nähte und die Verwendung von Abnähern ergibt sich die plastische Gestaltung.

1-2-3-4. Abnäher sind keilförmige, spitz auslaufende Falten, die in nicht-elastische Stoffe genäht werden. In der Grundschnittaufstellung haben sie ihren festen Platz. Während der Anprobe können die notwendigen Korrekturen an den Abnähern am besten vorgenommen werden. In der Modellschnittkonstruktion dagegen werden ihre Positionen meist verändert; sie „verschwinden" in Nähten, werden im Papierschnitt zugelegt oder so eingefügt, dass sie entweder gar nicht auffallen oder als dekoratives Element besonders zur Geltung kommen.

Möchte man einen Abnäher verschieben, so sollte man immer bedenken, dass er in seiner ursprünglichen Position der Körperform am ehesten entspricht. Deshalb sollte ein Abnäher in der Parallelverschiebung, wie beispielsweise der dargestellte

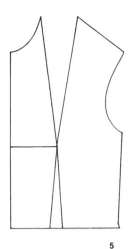
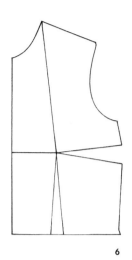
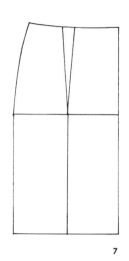
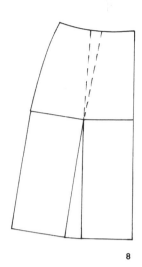

| 5 | 6 | 7 | 8 |

should be closed with the relevant fullness being taken up in the new dart. In its new position, the dart may appear to be wider or narrower on account of its new length, but there will be no change in its effect on the pattern.

7-8. The act of closing a dart can be used to remove it completely. However, just as happens when the dart is transferred, the fullness of the material is not lost but simply "moves" to another site. Unlike in the case of moving the dart, this volume of material is not sewn up. Instead, its width will be used to obtain a greater diameter or a thicker hem.

5-6. L'autre moyen pour modifier la position des pinces est de les transférer. Il convient d'abord de déterminer la nouvelle position de la pince et de la dessiner sur le papier dans sa nouvelle position. La pince d'origine sera fermée et le volume correspondant passera à la nouvelle pince. Dans sa nouvelle position, la pince peut sembler plus large o plus étroite, sa longueur étant modifiée, mais son effet sur le patron ne varie pas.

7-8. La fermeture d'une pince peut servir à la supprimer entièrement. Cependant, tout comme lors de son transfert, son volume ne se perd pas mais « passe » dans une autre direction. À la différence de ce qui se produit avec le déplacement, le volume ne sera pas cousu mais sa largeur sera utilisée pour obtenir un plus grand diamètre ou un ourlet plus épais.

Taillenabnäher, immer nur so weit wie unbedingt nötig von seinem Platz verlegt werden. Empfehlenswert ist es, diese Verschiebung auf 3 – 4 cm zu begrenzen.

5-6. Eine weitere Form, die Position von Abnähern zu verändern, ist das Verlegen. Zunächst wird die neue Position des Abnähers bestimmt und auf der so entstandenen Linie das Papier eingeschnitten. Der ursprüngliche Abnäher wird dann zugelegt und das entsprechende Volumen springt in den neuen Abnäher über. In seiner neuen Position kann der Abnäher durch die Veränderung seiner Länge breiter oder schmaler aussehen, der Effekt auf den Schnitt bleibt jedoch erhalten.

7-8. Das Zulegen eines Abnähers kann man auch vornehmen, um ihn ganz zu entfernen. Sein Volumen geht allerdings – genau wie bei der Verlegung – nicht verloren, sondern „springt" nur in eine andere Richtung. Im Unterschied zur Verlegung wird das Volumen allerdings nicht vernäht, sondern seine Weite genutzt, um zusätzliche Reihweite oder mehr Rocksaum zu gewinnen.

Creative patternmaking

At the beginning of the creative patternmaking process one has the idea of adapting the pattern, producing a perfect silhouette, resolving very specific details or a fabric or color concept, or perhaps just the satisfaction of wearing an exclusive garment.

When the germ of a design takes seed in the imagination, it is a good idea to start sketching before drawing the pattern. This will clarify the details and proportions. Designs often spring from inspiration based on existing images, photos or sketches of fashion, or totally random images culled from daily life.

If we want to reproduce a sketch or photo, it will be very useful to start by making a full analysis of it. Where do the lines of the bust, waist and hips end exactly? How do I adapt the proportions (often stylized) on my pattern to make it the right size? In the first place it is important to establish the relationship between the seam allowances and flat and curved sections, before tracing them on the paper. In the photos, the length, elbow or cuffs, wherever these are visible, can be examined for guidance purposes.

Making up a pattern for a garment always starts with the basic pattern. If this is correct, the shape control lines (the lines that give a model its special shape, or determine the position of the seam, and the pockets, darts, etc.) are drawn in. When the shape control lines are drawn and the proportions established, it should always be borne in mind that we are working on a two-dimensional surface to obtain a three-dimensional product. When viewed from the front, for instance, the section located between the side seam and the so-called vertical line of vision, i.e. the last visible edge, usually remains outside our line of sight. In a skirt, this usually means about 4 cm from the side seam.

Le patronage créatif

À la racine du patronage créatif se trouve l'idée d'obtenir une adaptation ou bien une silhouette parfaite, la solution à des détails très concrets et un concept soit de tissu, soit de couleur. Tout cela parvient à la satisfaction de porter un vêtement unique.

Quand l'idée d'un dessin germe dans l'imagination, il est recommandé de commencer à l'esquisser avant de se mettre à dessiner le patron. Ainsi les détails et proportions seront clairs. L'inspiration des dessins provient souvent d'images existantes, de photos ou d'esquisses de mode ou d'images du quotidien totalement fortuites.

Si nous souhaitons reproduire un dessin ou une photo, il nous sera utile de commencer à envisager une analyse exacte. Où terminent exactement les lignes de la poitrine, de la taille et de la hanche ? Comment est-ce que j'adapte les proportions (souvent stylisées) à mon patron grandeur nature ? Il est important de commencer par établir les rapports entre les tailles de coutures, les zones plates et courbes, avant de les fixer sur papier. Sur les photos, à titre d'observation, il est possible d'observer la longueur, le coude ou les poings, sous réserve qu'ils soient visibles.

Le patronage d'un vêtement commence toujours avec le patron de base. S'il est exact, les lignes de modèle (les lignes conférant au modèle sa forme spéciale, définissant la position de la couture, ainsi que celle des poches, pinces, etc.) sont dessinées. Lors du dessin des lignes de modèle et de l'établissement des proportions, il faut toujours tenir compte du fait que nous travaillons sur une surface bidimensionnelle pour obtenir un produit tridimensionnel. Sur une vue de face, par exemple, la zone située entre la couture latérale et ladite ligne de vision verticale, c'est à dire les dernières extrémités visibles, sont en général hors de notre vue. Sur une jupe, cela implique généralement environ 4 cm à partir de la couture latérale.

Die kreative Schnittentwicklung

Am Beginn der kreativen Schnittentwicklung steht die Idee – die einer besonderen Silhouette oder auch der perfekten Passform, ganz konkrete Detaillösungen als auch Stoff- bzw. Farbvorstellungen – oder vielleicht auch der Genuss, den das Tragen eines Unikats bereitet.

Wenn die Idee für einen Entwurf ganz in der Imagination entstand, empfiehlt es sich, sie vor Beginn der Schnitterstellung zu skizzieren. So werden Proportionen und Details klar. Oft entstehen Designs auch durch Inspiration bereits bestehender Bilder, etwa Modefotos, Modezeichnungen oder ganz zufällige Alltagsbilder.

Will man eine Zeichnung oder ein Foto nachempfinden, ist es sehr hilfreich, die Vorlage zuerst einer genauen Analyse zu unterziehen. Wo genau verlaufen Brust-, Taillen- und Hüftlinie? Wie setze ich die (oft stilisierten) Proportionen auf meinen Realmaßgrundschnitt um? Wichtig ist es, zunächst alle Maßverhältnisse von Nahtlagen, Flächen und Winkeln zueinander in Bezug zu setzen, bevor man sie festlegt. Bei Fotos kann man die Gesichtslänge, Ellenbogen oder Handgelenke, sofern sichtbar, zur Orientierung heranziehen.

Die Schnittentwicklung für ein Kleidungsstück beginnt immer mit dem Grundschnitt. Passt dieser, werden die Modelllinien eingezeichnet – die Linien, die dem Modell seine spezielle Form geben, die Lage der Nähte festlegen oder auch die Positionen von Abnähern, Taschen usw. Beim Einzeichnen der Modelllinien und Festlegen der Proportionen sollte man sich immer wieder bewusst machen, dass man auf einer zweidimensionalen Ebene an einem dreidimensionalen Produkt arbeitet. Bei einer Frontalansicht, zum Beispiel, verliert man auf diese Weise schnell den Bereich, der zwischen der Seitennaht und der senkrechten sogenannten Sichtlinie liegt, also der letzten sichtbaren Kante, aus den Augen. Bei einem Rock sind das ca. 4 cm ab der Seitennaht.

Defining the shape control lines is no easy task for those without any experience. Taking measurements of our body, or bust will give us confidence and train our eye. The relationship between the size of the technical mannequins, fashion sketches or photographs and the pattern can be calculated with the aid of some basic figures. To do so, first we measure the distance on the basic pattern between the waist and the base of the neck, e.g. 37 cm. Then the same distance on the model, e.g. 12 cm. If we divide 37 by 12, we get 3; that is to say, 1cm on the sample corresponds to 3 cm on our pattern. This calculation can also be used for relations regarding length. The silhouette and width are assessed proportionately. Here a great deal of precision is required, along with a tendency to opt for the average value, since when drawing patterns, we usually move imperceptibly between correcting our constructions and the real shape, logical deductions and the sense of the lines and proportions.

Good pattern designers know the importance of working with as much precision as possible, but neither do they forget that patterns need to be able to adapt to a three-dimensional figure with a flexible fabric. The body does not have any corners or completely straight lines. Consequently, we can only come close to reality using the pattern and this deficit should be counterbalanced by adjusting the garment directly to make it fit the body.

The same applies with the "tacit rules" of tailoring.

Our eyes and movements have become used to feminine garments, for example, closing from right to left, or side zippers and asymmetric decorative elements always being located on the left-hand side of the body. We should be aware of such conventions so as to be able to deal with them wherever necessary.

Pour ceux qui n'ont pas d'expérience, il n'est pas facile de déterminer les lignes de modèle. Prendre des mesures de notre corps ou de la poitrine nous donnera de la sécurité et nous aidera à habituer notre regard. Les rapports entre les tailles de mannequins techniques, les ébauches de mode ou les photos et patrons peuvent se calculer à l'aide de quelques chiffres de base. Pour ce faire, nous mesurons d'abord dans le patron de base la distance entre la taille et le col, par ex. 37 cm. Nous passons ensuite à la même distance dans le modèle, par ex. 12 cm. Si nous divisons 37 par 12, nous obtenons 3, c'est à dire que 1 cm de l'échantillon correspond à 3 cm sur notre patron. Ce calcul sert également pour les rapports de longueur. La silhouette et la largeur s'évaluent proportionnellement. Une grande précision et une disposition au juste milieu sont ici nécessaires puisque, dans le dessin de patrons, nous naviguons généralement de manière subtile entre la correction des constructions et la forme réelle, les déductions logiques et le sens des lignes et des proportions.

Les bons dessinateurs de patrons savent combien il est important de travailler le plus exactement possible mais ils n'oublient pas, d'un autre côté, que les patrons devront s'adapter au corps tridimensionnel avec un tissu souple. Le corps n'a pas de coins, ni de lignes totalement droites. C'est pour cette raison que le patron ne nous permettra que de nous rapprocher de la réalité et ce déficit devra s'équilibrer par une adaptation directe du vêtement au corps.

La même chose se produit avec les « lois tacites » du métier de tailleur.

Nos yeux et mouvements se sont habitués, par exemple, à ce que les vêtements féminins se ferment de droite à gauche ou à ce que les fermetures éclair latérales ou décorations asymétriques se trouvent toujours du côté gauche du corps. Nous devrions connaître ces conventions pour pouvoir y faire face lorsque cela sera nécessaire.

Das Festlegen von Modelllinien stellt für Ungeübte keine so leichte Aufgabe dar. Kontrollmessungen am eigenen Körper oder der Büste schaffen Sicherheit und schulen das Auge. Die Maßverhältnisse zwischen technischer Figurine, modischer Skizze oder Foto und dem Schnitt können auch mit Hilfe einer Basiszahl errechnet werden. Dazu misst man zuerst am Grundschnitt die Strecke von Taille zur Halsgrube, z. B. 37 cm, danach dieselbe Strecke an der Vorlage, z. B. 12 cm. Man dividiert dann 37 : 12 und erhält 3, d.h. 1 cm an der Figurine entspricht 3 cm im Schnitt. Diese Rechnung gilt für die Längenverhältnisse. Silhouette und Breitenmaße werden proportional geschätzt. Hier sind feines Austarieren und die Bereitschaft zu Kompromissen notwendig, denn beim Schnittzeichnen bewegt man sich oft auf einem feinen Grad zwischen der Korrektheit der Konstruktion und der wirklichen Form, den logischen Folgerungen und dem Gefühl für Linien und Proportionen.

Gute Schnittmacher wissen, wie wichtig es zum einen ist, so exakt wie möglich zu arbeiten, zum anderen aber nicht zu vergessen, dass Schnitte mit einem flexiblen Stoff an einem dreidimensionalen Körper umgesetzt werden. Der Körper hat weder Ecken noch schnurgerade Linien. Man kann sich daher mit dem Schnitt der Form nur annähern und muss dieses Defizit durch das direkte Anpassen des Kleidungsstücks an den Körper ausgleichen. Ähnlich verhält es sich es auch mit den „ungeschriebenen Gesetzen" der Kleidermacherei. Unsere Augen und Bewegungen haben sich daran gewöhnt, dass beispielsweise Frauenkleidung Rechts über Links schließt oder dass seitliche Verschlüsse und asymmetrische Dekorationen immer auf der linken Körperseite ihren Platz finden. Man sollte sich dieser traditionellen Konventionen bewusst werden, um sich ihnen dann bei Bedarf gezielt zu widersetzen.

Modeling

One continuous way to develop patterns creatively is to use the modeling technique. Here the fabric is placed on the tailor's bust and worked on directly, developing a specific shape or a whole garment, and thereby obtaining a unique piece from which the pattern can be drawn for the piece modeled, transferring the tracings and markings to paper.

Modeling is the direct, physical search for shapes, and this technique, involving practical experimentation and rejection, usually generates completely new ideas and designs. For many people, this procedure is simpler than the more intricate process of drawing patterns, as the result of each action can be seen immediately. On the other hand, there are others that find it really complicated to confront a piece of cloth directly, without having any lines to help them give it shape and transfer it on to a pattern.

Objective modeling clearly requires practice. Each individual should decide for themselves how they want to go about the process, where to place their pins and how to develop the shape without the fabric constantly sliding out of position, how the pieces will be cut and assembled, how the pieces will be stitched together to make the final paper pattern coincide exactly with the piece that has been modeled, and how we can ensure that the final model that is sewn up coincides with the real design.

In spite of its apparent complexity, modeling is a determining factor for understanding the skill of pattern making, and should be tested with at least a few practical exercises. For modeling purposes, we recommend selecting a sample fabric that hangs in more or less the same way as the target garment. It can also be helpful to mark the main contours of the body (neck circumference, bust, waist and hip circumference) on the mannequin, along with the main points (bust, points for insertion of the sleeves) by basting with

Modelage

Le modelage est une forme continue de développement créatif de patrons. Ici, on travaille directement sur le tissu sur le buste du tailleur, en développant une forme ou un vêtement tout entier et en obtenant une pièce unique, à partir de laquelle sera obtenu ensuite le patron de la pièce modelée, en transférant sur le papier des traits et marques.

Le modelage est une recherche de formes directe et physique et cette technique d'essais et d'éliminations donne lieu, en général, à des dessins et idées entièrement nouveaux. Pour beaucoup de gens, cette procédure est plus simple que le détour du dessin des patrons, puisque le résultat de chaque action est visible directement. À d'autres, au contraire, il semble très compliqué d'affronter directement une pièce de tissu, sans lignes d'aide, lui donner une forme et la transférer sur des patrons.

Le modelage objectif nécessite assurément de la pratique. Chacun doit penser par lui-même comment commencer le processus, où placer les aiguilles et comme la forme se développe sans déplacement continu du tissu de sa place, comment les pièces se coupent et se placent, comment les pièces s'assemblent de manière à ce que le patron en papier qui en résulte corresponde exactement à la pièce modelée et comment nous pouvons nous assurer que le modèle final cousu corresponde au dessin réel.

Malgré cette complexité apparente, le modelage est décisif pour la compression du patronage et quelques exercices pratiques devraient au moins être réalisés. Pour le modelage, il est recommandé de sélectionner un tissu d'essai avec une chute similaire à celle du vêtement souhaité. Il est également utile de marquer sur le mannequin les principales lignes de contour (tour de cou, de poitrine, de taille et de hanche) et les principaux points (point de la poitrine, points d'insertion de la manche) avec des bâtis de différentes

Modellieren

Eine weiterführende Form der kreativen Schnittentwicklung ist das Modellieren. Hier arbeitet man direkt mit dem Stoff an der Schneiderbüste eine Form oder ein ganzes Kleidungsstück heraus und erhält dadurch ein Unikat – es sei denn man nimmt im Nachhinein den Schnitt vom modellierten Teil ab, indem man Umrisse und Markierungen auf Schnittpapier überträgt.

Modellieren ist eine sehr direkte, sinnliche Formsuche, und oft findet man mit dieser Technik des praktischen Ausprobierens und Verwerfens zu ganz neuen Ideen und Entwürfen. Diese Vorgehensweise ist für viele erst einmal leichter als der Umweg über das Schnittzeichnen, da das Ergebnis jeder Handlung direkt sichtbar ist. Anderen wiederum fällt es sehr schwer, frei und ohne Hilfslinien ein Stück Stoff in Angriff zu nehmen, es in Form zu bringen und in Schnittteile zu übertragen.

Zielgerichtetes Modellieren ist ganz allgemein zweifellos eine Sache der Übung. Man muss für sich selbst herausfinden, wie man den Prozess beginnt, wo man die Nadeln steckt und wie die Form entwickelt, ohne dass der Stoff ständig von seinem Platz rutscht, wie man einschneidet und Stücke ansetzt, wie man die Teile so abnimmt, dass der entstehende Papierschnitt dem modellierten auch genau entspricht, und wie man schlussendlich sicher stellt, dass das nachgenähte Modell den eigentlichen Entwurf verkörpert.

Trotz dieser scheinbaren Komplexität ist das Modellieren für das Verständnis der Schnittarbeit sehr entscheidend und sollte zumindest mit einigen leichten Übungen ausprobiert werden. Es empfiehlt sich für die Modellierung einen Probestoff zu wählen, der ähnlich fällt wie der des gewünschten Kleidungsstücks. Hilfreich ist es auch, auf der Büste die wichtigsten Umfangslinien (Halsansatzumfang, Brustumfang, Taillenumfang, Hüftumfang) und Punkte (Brustpunkt, Ärmeleinsatzzeichen) mit kontrastfarbigem Faden zu markieren

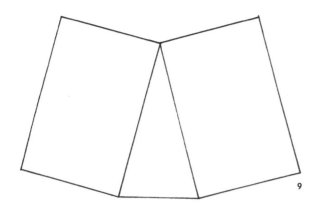

9

10

different colors of thread and transferring these to the model before removing it from the mannequin. Using these reference points it is possible to transfer the new shape control lines to a basic pattern.

When modeling and draping the cloth, the complexity of the relationship can be perceived between the body, fabric, and shape, and we see that the mystery of design is nothing more than playing around with basic geometrical shapes such as straight lines, circles, curves, right angles and triangles. For instance, if we try to draw the basic pattern from a fabric with right angles on the tailor mannequin, we will soon realize that in order to give shape to the fabric, we will need to use darts in some parts, i.e. the fabric forms a crease and the edge drops down.

9-10. The triangle is seen again in the outline of V necks or in the V-formations created in a pleated skirt. When the pieces in the pattern are "inverted", i.e. by cutting and turning them round the other way, this triangular shape is used to obtain more volume. The triangular formations that are for example included along the hem often turn out to be very useful.

11-12-13-14-15. Twists and turns are modeling practices that are slightly more advanced, and require soft fabrics that have a little give. Two pieces with their corresponding shape are twisted together and in so doing, the excess cloth becomes bunched up.

couleurs et de les déplacer sur le modèle avant de les extraire du mannequin. Avec ces points de référence, il est possible de transférer les nouvelles lignes de modèle sur un patron de base.

Le modelage et drapage permettent d'expérimenter la complexité du rapport entre corps, tissus et forme et de comprendre que tout le mystère de la conception n'est autre qu'un jeu entre des formes géométriques de base, comme des lignes droites, des cercles, des courbes, des angles droits et des triangles. Si, par exemple, nous essayons de dessiner le patron de base à partir d'une toile avec des angles droits sur le mannequin du tailleur, nous nous rendrons rapidement compte que, pour donner une forme au tissu, il est nécessaire d'utiliser des pinces sur certaines zones, c'est à dire, que le tissu fait un pli et laisse tomber l'extrémité.

9-10. Nous retrouvons le triangle dans la silhouette, dans les cols en V ou dans les coins créés dans un faux plissé. En « intervertissant » les pièces du patron, c'est à dire en les coupant et en les tournant en sens contraire, cette forme triangulaire est utilisée pour obtenir plus de volume. Les coins triangulaires qui, par exemple, sont également inclus dans la lisière, sont utiles à de nombreuses occasions.

11-12-13-14-15. Les liaisons et les tours sont des pratiques de modelage un peu plus avancées. Pour ce faire, des tissus doux qui s'étirent un peu sont requis. Deux pièces avec leur forme correspondante tournent entre elles et, de ce fait, l'excès de tissu forme les plis.

und auf das Modell zu übertragen, bevor es von der Büste genommen wird. Anhand dieser Anhaltspunkte können die neuen Modelllinien auch auf einem Grundschnitt eingetragen werden.

Beim Modellieren und Drapieren erfährt man unmittelbar die Vielfältigkeit des Zusammenspiels von Körper, Stoff und Form und versteht, dass das ganze Geheimnis des Entwurfs eigentlich nichts anderes ist als ein Zusammenspiel geometrischer Grundformen, wie Geraden, Rundungen, Winkel, Rechtecke, Kreise und Dreiecke. Versucht man zum Beispiel den Grundschnitt aus einem rechteckigen Stoff an der Schneiderbüste herauszumodellieren, bemerkt man sehr schnell, dass man zur Formung des Stoffes an bestimmten Stellen Abnäher anbringen muss, d.h. den Stoff in eine Falte legt und spitz auslaufen lässt.

9-10. Das Dreieck findet man in der Silhouette, als V-Ausschnitt oder auch eingesetzten Keil bei einem Faltenrock wieder. Beim „Aufdrehen" von Schnittteilen, also dem Einschneiden und Auseinanderdrehen, nutzt man diese dreieckige Form, um zusätzliches Volumen zu gewinnen. Dreieckige Keile, die beispielsweise in den Saum eingefügt werden, verhelfen so zu einem größeren Umfang.

11-12-13-14-15. Verschlingungen und Verdrehungen sind schon etwas fortgeschrittenere Modellierübungen. Hierfür eignen sich weiche Stoffe mit etwas Dehnfähigkeit. Zwei geformte Teile werden miteinander verdreht, die Stofffülle wird an der Verdrehung in Falten gelegt.

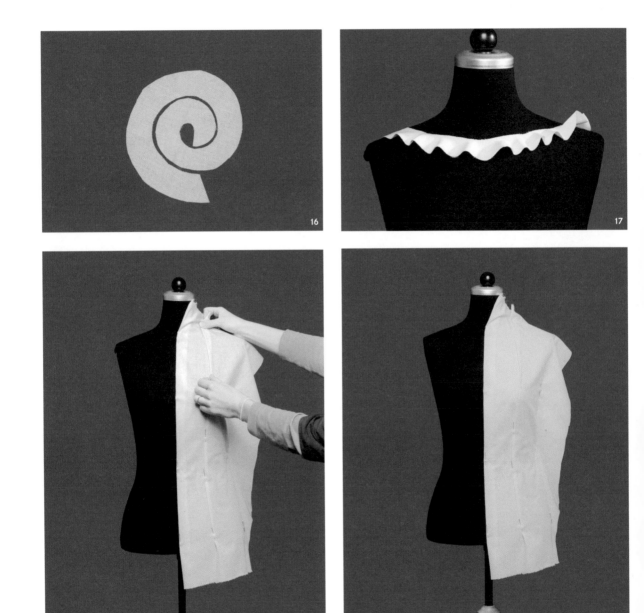

16-17. A circle with a hole and a spiral are typical because the outer diameter is always greater than the inner one and it is in this way that we can get a skirt to hang well, for example. The spiral creates waves, which can be used as flounces (artistic decorative items that fall in the shape of a bell), for example.

18-19. When placing the fabric on the mannequin, make sure that the straight grain of the fabric is vertical, in other words, that it flows parallel to the front center and back center lines. Thus, the fibers that run crosswise should always remain horizontal on the bust and shoulder blades. If for example the straight grain of the fabric needs to be transferred to a roll of fabric, we should line it up with the selvage or pull on a thread in the fabric. If the darts are hidden, it should be possible to drape the fabric around the mannequin without it creasing or stretching anywhere.
Direct work on the tailor bust or on the model is essential to check the volume and silhouettes, as well as the collar, pockets and sleeves, or to see if it is the right shape.

16-17. Un cercle avec un orifice et une spirale se caractérisent par un diamètre extérieur toujours supérieur à l'intérieur, ce qui permet d'obtenir, par exemple, la chute d'une jupe. La spirale crée des ondes, qui peuvent être utilisées, par ex., comme des volants (décorations en plastique avec chute en forme de cloche).

18-19. Au moment de placer le tissu sur le mannequin, il faut faire attention que la direction du fil du tissu soit verticale, c'est à dire qu'elle avance parallèlement au milieu avant et au milieu du dos. Les fibres transversales doivent toujours rester ainsi horizontales sur la poitrine et les omoplates. Par exemple, pour transmettre la direction du fil à un rouleau de tissu, nous devrons regarder la lisière ou tirer d'un fil du tissu. Si les pinces sont dissimulées, le tissu devrait entourer le mannequin sans faire de plis et sans être étiré.
Le travail direct sur le buste du tailleur ou sur le modèle est indispensable pour vérifier le volume et les silhouettes, ainsi que le cou, les poches et les manches, ou bien pour voir si la forme est adaptée.

16-17. Ein Kreis mit Loch und eine Spirale haben die Eigenschaft, dass der äußere Kreis immer mehr Umfang aufweist als der innere, und so erhält zum Beispiel der Kreisrock seinen besonderen Fall. Die Spirale bildet Wellen, die z. B. als sogenannte „Volants" – glockig fallende, plastische Verzierungen – Verwendung finden.

18-19. Beim Anlegen des Stoffs an die Büste muss man darauf achten, dass der Fadenlauf senkrecht ausgerichtet ist, also parallel zur Vorderen und Hinteren Mitte verläuft. Die Querfäden sollten dabei immer waagerecht über Brust und Schulterblättern liegen. Will man den Fadenlauf in einem Stoffballen ermitteln, orientiert man sich an der Webkante oder zieht einen Faden aus dem Gewebe. Wenn die Abnäher gesteckt sind, sollte der Stoff die Büste faltenlos umgeben und nicht spannen.
Die direkte Arbeit an der Schneiderbüste oder am Modell ist unerlässlich, um Volumen und Silhouetten, aber auch Kragen, Taschen und Ärmel, auzutesten oder die Passform zu überprüfen.

The practice of drawing patterns

For practical reasons, we recommend you start by following the directions using the exact measurements and then use the basic pattern for your own creations. When the basic patterns are perfect, and the fabric samples have been approved and modified, the best prerequisites will have been established for experimenting with the pattern configuration without any constraints, there remaining a strong likelihood that the pattern obtained will also need to be adapted.

Finally, you can try and work with the model patterns. As the body is mostly symmetrical, in basic patterns and most model patterns, only one half is drawn. In other words, working with the measurements for half of the body circumference - from the center front to the center back - is sufficient. Before cutting the fabric, this should be folded and laid double, so that the center front or center back of the pattern piece coincides exactly with the line along which the fabric is folded. In the industrial sector and in the case of asymmetric patterns, the whole pattern is drawn, as it is not cut with the fabric folded double.

The right angle between the center front and the center back, and also in all the joining areas, is extremely important since there should be no stitches or holes visible when the fabric is unfolded or the pieces are sewn together. Consequently, when the pattern is being made up, all the pieces should be joined at their seams and checked.

When the pattern pieces are ready, it is essential to label them in order. Numbering helps to see the whole set at a glance and

La pratique du dessin de patrons

Pour des raisons pratiques, il est recommandé de commencer par suivre les indications avec les mesures exactes pour élaborer ensuite les créations sur le patron de base. Une fois les patrons de base parfaits avec les prototypes sur tissu déjà essayés et modifiés, nous aurons défini les conditions préalables les plus adaptées pour une expérimentation sans limites, avec la configuration de patrons et toujours une grande probabilité de ce que le patron obtenu soit aussi adapté.

Pour finir, il est possible de se lancer au travail avec des patrons de modèle. Étant donné que le corps (dans sa plus grande partie) est symétrique, seule est dessinée une moitié sur les patrons de base et la plupart des patrons de modèle, c'est à dire avec la moitié des mesures de tour, qui sont suffisantes du milieu avant au milieu du dos. Avant de couper la toile, il faut la placer en double afin que le milieu avant ou le milieu du dos de la pièce du patron se trouve exactement sur la ligne où le tissu est plié. Dans le secteur industriel et pour les patrons asymétriques, les patrons sont dessinés au complet puisque la coupe ne s'effectue pas en double.

L'angle droit entre le milieu avant et le milieu du dos, ainsi que dans toutes les zones d'assemblage, est d'une extrême importance, afin que lors de l'ouverture de la toile en double ou lors de l'assemblage, il n'y ait pas de pointe, ni d'espace. Pour ce faire, pendant l'élaboration du patron, toutes les pièces devraient être assemblées par les coutures et comparées.

Une fois les pièces du patron prêtes, une composition de texte ordonnée est

Praktisches zum Schnittzeichnen

Es empfiehlt sich aus praktischen Gründen, mit den Anleitungen zum exakten Maßnehmen zu beginnen, um sich dann die Grundschnittkonstruktionen zu erarbeiten. Sind die Grundschnitte erst einmal perfekt, mit Prototypen aus Stoff probiert und abgeändert, hat man die besten Voraussetzungen für grenzenloses Herumexperimentieren mit der Schnittgestaltung geschaffen, stets mit der hohen Wahrscheinlichkeit, dass der entstandene Schnitt auch passt.

Im Anschluss daran, kann man sich an die Arbeit mit den Modellschnitten wagen. Da der Körper (weitestgehend) symmetrisch ist, werden Grundschnitte und die meisten Modellschnitte als halber Umfang gezeichnet, d. h. man arbeitet mit den halben Umfangmaßen, die von der Vorderen bis zur Hinteren Mitte reichen. Der Stoff wird beim Zuschnitt in den Bruch, also doppelt, gelegt, wobei die Vordere oder Hintere Mitte des Schnittteils genau auf dem Bruch liegen muss. In der Industrie und bei asymmetrischen Schnitten werden die Schnitte komplett gezeichnet, da der Zuschnitt nicht paarweise erfolgt.

Der rechte Winkel an Vorderer und Hinterer Mitte sowie an allen Anschlussstellen ist enorm wichtig, damit beim Aufklappen des Bruchs oder Zusammensetzen der Teile keine Spitzen und Dellen entstehen. Man sollte daher bei der Schnitterstellung alle Schnittteile an den Nähten zusammenlegen und ausgleichen.

Wenn die Schnittteile fertig sind, ist eine ordentliche Beschriftung essentiell. Eine Durchnummerierung sorgt für Überblick und hilft dabei, dass kein noch so kleines

avoid any small pieces getting lost. Marking the straight grain of the fabric guarantees that each pattern piece will be cut out along the correct line.

Providing directions, such as indicating how many times a piece should be cut out (twice for the same piece or once with the fabric folded double) or if it should be reinforced with interfacing, minimizes the possibility of error and makes cutting out that much faster.

The exact marking of the pieces and joining points (crosswise lines) on the edges of the patterns, such as for example along the line marking the bust, waist and hips, the sleeve inset markers, the positions of the darts and the width of the seam allowance, will make it easier to read the pattern. With this aim in mind, in drawing patterns letters and special markings are also used, and you should become familiar with these over time. A short list of standard markings is provided below:

fondamentale. La numérotation aide à voir l'ensemble en un seul coup d'œil et à éviter de perdre de petites pièces. Le marquage de la direction du fil nous garantit que chaque pièce du patron sera coupée avec le bon alignement.

Les indications, comme le nombre de fois où une pièce doit être coupée (deux fois la même ou une fois avec la toile en double) ou le renfort ou non avec une triplure, minimisent les sources d'erreurs et accélèrent en grande mesure la coupe.

Le marquage exact des pièces et points d'assemblage (symboles transversaux) sur les bords des patrons comme, par ex, la ligne de la poitrine, de la taille et des hanches, les marques d'insertion des manches, les positions des pinces et la largeur des ajouts de couture, autorise ensuite la lecture du patron. Dans ce but, des lettres et des marques spéciales auxquelles il faut s'habituer avec le temps sont utilisées dans le dessin de patrons. Voici maintenant une petite sélection de marques standards :

Teil verloren gehen kann. Die Einzeichnung des Fadenlaufs stellt sicher, dass jedes Schnittteil im Anschluss mit der richtigen Ausrichtung zugeschnitten wird.

Angaben, wie oft ein Teil zugeschnitten werden muss, also etwa paarweise, oder ob es im Bruch liegt oder mit Einlagen verstärkt werden soll, minimieren die Fehlerquellen und beschleunigen den Zuschnitt enorm.

Die genaue Markierung der Teile und Ansatzpunkte (Querzeichen) an den Schnitträndern, so z. B. Brust-, Taillen- und Hüftlinie, die Ärmeleinsatzzeichen, Abnäherpositionen und Nahtzugabenbreite, ermöglicht es auch zu einem späteren Zeitpunkt, aber auch Außenstehenden, den Schnitt zu lesen. Zu diesem Zweck werden beim Schnittzeichnen auch spezielle Zeichen und Bezeichnungen benutzt, die man sich im Laufe der Zeit angewöhnen sollte. Im Folgenden ist eine kleine Auswahl an Standardbezeichnungen aufgelistet:

ÄB % 0-3 cm	↓	⌐	⅄	X ⫴ O	C.F. ON FOLD
The % and - symbols differ from standard math usage. In pattern drawing they stand respectively for "minus" and "up until".	The arrow shows the straight grain of the fabric.	This symbol indicates a right angle.	A cross on a dart means that it is to be omitted.	In pleats, an arrow indicates the direction of the pleat. For the sake of clarity, an X may also be used together with an O. The shaded areas are omitted or transformed.	C.F. and C.B. indicate the center front and center back. "On Fold" or "Double" means that the piece should be cut out with the fabric folded double.
Contrairement à l'habituel, dans le dessin de patrons le symbole % dans una formule s'interprete comme «moins», et le trait d'union comme «jusqu'à».	La flèche marque la direction du fil.	Ce symbole indique un angle droit.	Une croix sur une pince signifie qu'elle va être omise.	Sur les plis, une flèche indique la direction du pli. Pour que ce soit plus clair, il est aussi possible d'utiliser le symbole X joint à un O. Les zones ombrées sont omises ou transformées.	C.F. et C.B ou Mav et Mdo indiquent le milieu avant et le milieu du dos. On Fold ou double signifie que la pièce doit être coupée sur un tissu en double.
Das in den Formeln benutzte Prozentzeichen bedeut im Schnittzeichnen, anders als üblich, „minus", der Bindestrich „bis".	Ein Pfeil gibt die Richtung des Fadenlaufs an.	Dieses Zeichen indiziert einen rechten Winkel.	Ein Kreuz über einem Abnäher bedeutet, dass er wegfällt.	Bei Falten bezeichnet ein Pfeil die Legerichtung; zur weiteren Verdeutlichung kann auch das Symbol X eingezeichnet werden, das zu O gelegt wird. Schraffierte Abschnitte fallen weg oder werden zugelegt.	C.F. und C.B. oder VM und HM bezeichnen die Vordere und Hintere Mitte. On Fold oder Bruch sagt aus, dass das Teil auf einem doppelt gelegten, zusammenhängenden Stoff zugeschnitten werden muss.

Taking measurements

If you want to create patterns tailored to the measurements and characteristics of a specific body, this should be measured carefully. A pattern that is made to measure, fitted and adjusted is perfectly adapted to the needs of an individual body, and can enhance the attractive parts and hide the defects.

Two people are always needed when taking measurements, since the person that is going to be measured should remain in a natural, upright position. We can take measurements of a person dressed in their underwear or a thin dress, but not in a sweater or jeans, since these will have a significant effect on the results of the measurements. Where very accurate measurements are required, such as a corset, for example, for a wedding dress, always wearing the same bra – from the first measurement to the last – is recommended.

Before taking measurements and creating the pattern, the body should be observed and drawn with accuracy and from various angles. We should pay special attention to how the contours of the body are distributed, its various curves and any deviations from the norm that are visible when working with the pattern. All measurements should be taken with the measuring tape snug against the body, making sure it is not too tight or too loose.

20-21. The best thing is to start with a waist tape, i.e. a tape measure with hooks at the ends to close it and be able to pass it round the waist and hook it together in the right place. The waist circumference (WAC) should be kept right at the narrowest part of the trunk throughout the entire measuring process.

22-23-24. The next thing to be measured is the bust circumference (BC). This is done by placing the measuring tape over the uppermost part of the bust and round the body, passing under the arms and up a bit over the shoulder blades.

25. The hip circumference (HC) is the horizontal circumference of the body measured at the widest part of the bottom. The best way to take this measurement is from the side.

Prise de mesures

Pour créer des patrons adaptés aux mesures et caractéristiques d'un corps précis, celui-ci doit être soigneusement mesuré. Un patron sur mesure essayé et corrigé s'ajuste exactement aux besoins d'un corps individuel et peut rehausser ses zones les plus belles ou cacher ses défauts. Pour prendre des mesures, deux personnes seront nécessaires car celle qui va être mesurée doit être en position debout et naturelle. La prise de mesure peut s'effectuer en sous-vêtements ou avec un vêtement fin mais pas avec un pull et un jean car cela influerait beaucoup sur les résultats de la mesure. Si des mesures très précises sont nécessaires comme, par exemple, pour un corset de robe de mariage, il est recommandé de toujours porter le même soutien-gorge, de la première mesure au dernier essai.

Avant la prise de mesure et la création du patron, le corps doit être observé et dessiné avec précision et depuis plusieurs perspectives. Nous devons nous intéresser spécialement à la manière dont les contours se répartissent sur le corps, aux courbes qu'il présente ou aux écarts par rapport à la norme qui peuvent s'apprécier dès le travail avec le patron. Toutes les mesures doivent être prises avec le mètre collé au corps mais ni trop étiré, ni trop lâche.

20-21. Il vaut mieux commencer avec un mètre pour la taille, c'est à dire un mètre avec des crochets à ses extrémités pour pouvoir le fermer, et avec lui la ceinture, en fermant les crochets au bon endroit. Au cours de la mesure, le tour de taille (TT) devrait se prendre exactement dans la zone la plus étroite du tronc.

22-23-24. Ce qui se mesure ensuite, c'est le tour de poitrine (TP). Pour ce faire, le mètre ruban doit être placé devant la zone la plus haute de la poitrine et il faut faire le tour du corps en passant sous les bras et en l'élevant un peu dans la zone des omoplates.

25. Le tour de hanches (TH) est le contour horizontal du corps mesuré dans la zone la plus large de l'arrière. Il vaut mieux prendre cette mesure depuis une position latérale.

Maßnehmen

Wenn man Schnitte anfertigen möchte, die speziell auf die Maße und Eigenheiten eines bestimmten Körpers abgestimmt sind, muss dieser sehr sorgfältig wahrgenommen und vermessen werden. Ein probierter und korrigierter Maßschnitt folgt genau den Bedürfnissen eines individuellen Körpers und kann dessen Vorteile noch hervorheben oder Defizite an anderer Stelle kaschieren.

Fürs Maßnehmen werden immer zwei Personen benötigt, da diejenige, der das Maß abgenommen wird, eine aufrechte, natürliche Haltung annehmen soll. Das Vermessen kann über der Unterwäsche oder einem leichten Kleid geschehen, nicht aber über Pulli und Jeans, da diese die Messergebnisse beträchtlich beeinflussen würden. Im Falle ganz genauer Maßanfertigungen, wie z. B. einer Korsage für ein Hochzeitskleid, ist es empfehlenswert, von der ersten Messung bis zur letzten Anprobe immer den gleichen BH zu tragen.

Vor dem Maßnehmen und der Schnitterstellung sollte der Körper genau und aus mehreren Perspektiven betrachtet und skizziert werden. Man sollte sein Augenmerk besonders darauf richten, wie sich die Umfangsmaße auf den Körper verteilen, welche Rundungen der Körper aufweist oder welche Abweichungen von der Norm schon in der Schnittarbeit berücksichtigt werden können. Alle Maße müssen glatt am Körper, also nicht zu eng und nicht zu locker genommen werden.

20-21. Zu Beginn legt man am besten ein Taillenband, also ein Maßband, an dessen Enden Häkchen zum Schließen angebracht sind, um die Taille und lässt das Häkchen an entsprechender Stelle einhaken. Der Taillenumfang (TU) sollte während der gesamten Messungen gerade um die schmalste Stelle des Rumpfes liegen.

22-23-24. Als nächstes wird der Brustumfang (BU) ermittelt. Hierbei wird das Maßband vorne von der höchsten Stelle der Büste ausgehend, unter den Armen durchgeführt und leicht nach oben über die Schulterblätter gelegt.

25. Der Hüftumfang (HU) ist der waagerecht gemessene Umfang des Körpers im Bereich der stärksten Stelle des Gesäßes. Am besten wird das Maß von einer seitlichen Position aus genommen.

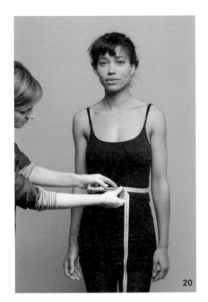

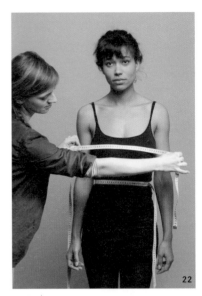

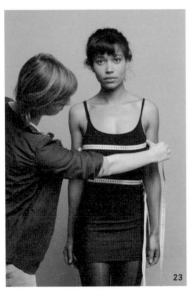

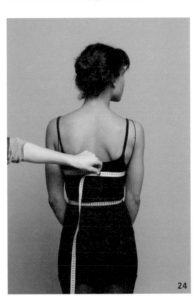

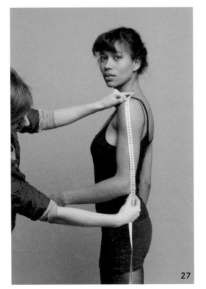

26. The distance between the hip circumference (HC) and the waist circumference is the hip depth (HD), which is usually measured from the waist down and is about 19–22 cm.

27-28. The next thing to measure is the shoulder width (SW), sleeve length (SL) and the position of the elbow. The shoulder width is obtained by running the measuring tape from the base of the neck to the shoulder bone. If we measure from here to the outer point of the elbow, this will give us its position. If we measure from the shoulder bone to the wrist, this will give us the length of the sleeve.
With very thick or very thin arms, we also need to measure the circumference of the arm and forearm.

29. The measurement of the back height (BAH) determines the position and depth of the armhole. To obtain this value, we need to place a strip of paper underneath the arm, reaching the spinal column. Starting at the top of the spine, extend the measuring tape to the upper end of the horizontal strip of paper, so as to be able to see the back height.

30. The back length (BL) should also be measured from the top of the spine, but this time extending the tape to the lower side of the waist circumference. The back length, together with the front length, is one of the most important measurements. This value should be measured with extreme accuracy, and checked against the measuring chart. If the value measured differs widely from the measuring chart, as a beginner the best thing is to use the values given in the table.

31. The back width (BAW) should be measured roughly at the height of the bust circumference, at the bottom of the shoulder blade. It should be measured flat across the back from one armhole to the other, marking two big creases where the back is to be joined to the sleeves, with the arms hanging limp by the side of the body.

32. The next thing is to place the measuring tape at the front, at the base of the neck. The bust depth (BD) should be measured to the fullest part of the bust, and the front length (FL) to the lower waist line.

26. La distance entre le tour de hanches (TH) et le tour de taille est la longueur taillle-bassin (LTB), qui doit être d'environ 19-22 cm de la taille jusqu'en bas.

27-28. Il faut mesurer ensuite la longueur d'épaule (LE), la longueur de manche (LoM) et l'emplacement du coude. La largeur d'épaule s'obtient en plaçant le mètre ruban de la base du cou jusqu'à l'os de l'épaule. Si nous mesurons d'ici jusqu'au point extérieur du coude, nous obtiendrons sa position. Depuis l'os de l'épaule, si nous mesurons jusqu'au poignet, nous obtiendrons la longueur de manche.
Pour des bras très gros ou très maigres, il faudra prendre aussi la mesure du tour de bras et d'avant-bras.

29. Le mesure de la hauteur du dos (HD) détermine la position et la profondeur de l'orifice pour la manche. Pour obtenir cette valeur, nous devrons placer une bande de papier sous le bras jusqu'à la colonne vertébrale. En commençant par la vertèbre cervicale supérieure, le mètre ruban sera étendu jusqu'à l'extrémité supérieure de la bande de papier horizontal, afin de voir ainsi la hauteur d'épaule.

30. La longueur du dos (LD) se mesurera également de la vertèbre cervicale supérieure, mais jusqu'à l'extrémité inférieure du tour de taille cette fois. La longueur du dos, avec la longueur de devant, figure parmi les mesures les plus importantes. Cette valeur doit se mesurer très précisément et se comparer avec le tableau de mesures. En cas d'écarts importants entre la valeur mesurée et la table de mesures, en tant que débutant, il vaut mieux utiliser les valeurs du tableau.

31. La carrure dos (CD) se mesurera environ à la hauteur du tour de poitrine, dans la zone inférieure de l'omoplate. Il faut la mesurer à plat à partir d'une entrée de manche jusqu'à l'autre et, avec les bras pendant naturellement, deux gros plis seront marqués pour déterminer l'assemblage entre le dos et les bras.

32. Dans l'étape suivante, nous placerons le mètre ruban sur la partie avant, à la base du cou. La profondeur de poitrine (PP) se mesurera directement jusqu'à l'extrémité de la poitrine et la longueur de devant (LDe) jusqu'à la ligne inférieure de la taille.

26. Der Abstand des Hüftumfangs (HU) zum Taillenring ist die Hüfttiefe (HT), die im Durchschnitt 19 – 22 cm unter der Taille liegt.

27-28. Als Nächstes werden die ungefähre Schulterbreite (SCHB), die Ärmellänge (ÄLG) und die Lage des Ellenbogens ermittelt. Die Schulterbreite erhält man, indem man das Maßband von der Halsansatzlinie bis zum Schulterknochen führt; misst man dann weiter bis zum äußeren Punkt des Ellenbogens, ergibt sich seine Position. Wenn man dann noch bis zur Handwurzel das Maß nimmt, so hat man die Ärmellänge. Bei sehr starken oder sehr schmalen Oberarmen sollte man auch die Umfangsmaße an Ober - und Unterarm erfassen.

29. Das Maß der Rückenhöhe (RH) bestimmt die Lage bzw. Tiefe des Armlochs. Diesen Wert erhält man, indem man einen Streifen Papier in die Armhöhle legt, der bis zur Wirbelsäule reicht. Nachdem der oberste Halswirbel ertastet worden ist, wird das Maßband von dort bis an die obere Kante des waagerechten Papierstreifens geführt und die Rückenhöhe abgelesen.

30. Die Rückenlänge (RL) wird ebenfalls vom obersten Halswirbelpunkt ab gemessen, und zwar bis zur unteren Kante des Taillenrings. Die Rückenlänge ist wie auch die Vorderlänge eines der wichtigsten Haltungsmaße. Dieser Wert muss sehr genau gemessen und mit der Maßtabelle überprüft werden. Bei größeren Abweichungen zwischen dem gemessenen Wert und der Tabelle sollte man sich als Anfänger auf die Werte der Maßtabelle stützen.

31. Die Rückenbreite (RB) wird ungefähr in Höhe der Brustumfangslinie im unteren Bereich der Schulterblätter ermittelt. Man misst glatt von Armansatz zu Armansatz, der bei hängenden Armen durch zwei scharfe Falten markiert wird, die den Abschluss zwischen Rücken und Armen bilden.

32. Im nächsten Schritt wird das Maßband von der Vorderseite aus an den Halswirbelpunkt gelegt. Die Brusttiefe (BT) wird direkt auf der Brustspitze abgelesen, die Vorderlänge (VL) am unteren Band des Taillenrings.

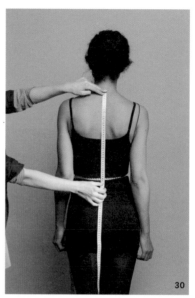

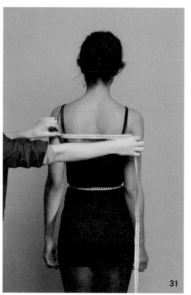

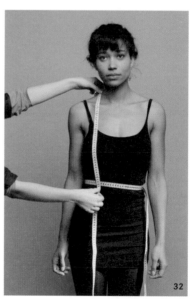

The measurements taken should be compared with the measuring chart and related to a pattern size. To do this we should use the bust circumference (BC) as a guide, selecting the pattern size that is closest to our bust circumference. We might find that the other measurements fail to coincide with those on the list, and that some measurements are missing. Why? The main measurements for body height (KH), bust circumference (BH), waist circumference (WAC), hip circumference (HC) and sleeve length (SL) should always be measured with the measuring tape snug against the body, and used directly on the pattern. On the other hand, the other measurements, i.e. the back height (BAH), back length (BL), hip depth (HD), bust depth (BD), front length (FL), back width (BAW) should be measured and compared with the values shown on the measuring chart. If there is any doubt, as a beginner, you should use the measurement given in the chart as your basis to start with, so as to eliminate most measuring errors.

The collar (C), armhole diameter (AD) and bust width (BW) should always be calculated as these are difficult measurements and the risk of making a mistake is very high. These measurements can be calculated with the aid the following formulas (based on a bust circumference BC of 80 cm).

C Collar

1/10 of 1/2 BU + 2 cm

AD Armhole diameter

1/8 BU % 1.5 cm

BW Bust width

1/4 BU % 4 cm

Once the relevant measurements have been calculated, you can continue making up the pattern. When doing this, it should be borne in mind that, in order to allow a certain freedom of movement in the garment, it is important to respect extra for the back height (BAH), back width (BAW), armhole diameter (AD) and bust width (BW), as well as the bust circumference (BC).

Such extra will depend on the specific model, material used, and the dress taste of the person concerned, but in any case here are some values that can be used for guidance:

Les mesures prises seront comparées avec le tableau de mesures et rapportées à une taille de confection. Pour ce faire, nous nous baserons sur le tour de poitrine (TP) et choisirons la taille de confection la plus proche de notre tour de poitrine. Il peut arriver que nous nous rendions compte que les autres résultats de mesure ne correspondent pas à ceux de la liste et qu'il manque quelques mesures. Pourquoi ? Les principales mesures de stature (S), tour de poitrine (TP), tour de taille (TT), tour de hanches (TH) et longueur de manche (LoM) doivent toujours être mesurées avec le mètre collé au corps et elles seront directement utilisées dans le patron. Au contraire, les mesures supplémentaires, c'est à dire la hauteur du dos (HD), la longueur du dos (LD), la longueur taillle-bassin (LTB), la profondeur de poitrine (PP), la longueur de devant (LDe), la carrure de dos (CD) seront mesurées et comparées avec le tableau de mesures. En cas de doute, en tant que débutant, vous devez vous baser tout d'abord sur la mesure du tableau pour éliminer la plupart des défauts de mesure.

Le col (C), le diamètre d'emmanchure (DE) et la largeur de poitrine (LP) se calculeront toujours car il s'agit de mesures difficiles et le risque de les réaliser de manière incorrecte est très élevé. À l'aide des formules suivantes, nous pouvons calculer ces mesures (à partir d'un TP de 80 cm).

C Col

1/10 de 1/2 TP + 2 cm

DE Diamètre d'emmanchure
1/8 TP % 1,5 cm

LP Largeur de poitrine

1/4 TP % 4 cm

Après avoir calculé les mesures pertinentes, il est possible de continuer la confection du patron. Pour ce faire, il faut tenir compte du fait que, pour permettre une certaine liberté de mouvements dans le vêtement, il est important de respecter les marges de hauteur du dos (HD), largeur du dos (LD), diamètre d'emmanchure (DE) et largeur de poitrine (LP), ainsi que le tour de poitrine (TP).

Les marges dépendent du modèle correspondant, du matériel utilisé et des préférences d'habillement de chacun mais, en tout cas, voici quelques valeurs indicatives.

Die ermittelten Maße werden nun mit der Maßtabelle verglichen und einer Konfektionsgröße zugeordnet. Dabei richtet man sich nach dem Brustumfang (BU), wählt also die Konfektionsgröße, die dem gemessenen Brustumfang am Nächsten kommt. Es kann nun sein, dass man feststellt, dass alle anderen Messergebnisse nicht mit denen auf der Liste übereinstimmen und noch einige Maße fehlen. Woran liegt das? Die Hauptmaße Körperhöhe (KH), Brustumfang (BU), Taillenumfang (TU), Hüftumfang (HU) und Ärmellänge (ÄLG) werden immer glatt am Körper gemessen und direkt für den Schnitt verwendet. Die Hilfsmaße dagegen, also Rückenhöhe (RH), Rückenlänge (RL), Hüfttiefe (HT), Brusttiefe (BT), Vorderlänge (VL), Rückenbreite (RB) werden gemessen und dann mit der Größentabelle verglichen. Im Zweifelsfall sollte man sich als Anfänger eher auf die Maße der Tabelle stützen, um grobe Fehlmessungen auszuschließen.

Halsspiegel (HS), Armlochdurchmesser (AD) und Brustbreite (BB) werden immer berechnet, weil diese Maße schwierig zu messen sind und das Risiko von fehlerhaften Messungen sehr hoch ist. Mit Hilfe folgender Formeln, kann man die Maße rechnerisch ermitteln (ab einem BU von 80 cm).

HS Halsspiegel

1/10 des 1/2 BU + 2 cm

AD Armlochdurchmesser

1/8 BU % 1,5 cm

BB Brustbreite

1/4 BU % 4 cm

Hat man die relevanten Maße ermittelt, kann im Folgenden mit der Schnittaufstellung begonnen werden. Es sollte dabei bedacht werden, dass, um einen gewissen Bewegungsspielraum im Kleidungsstück zu ermöglichen, die jeweiligen Zugaben an Rückenhöhe (RH), Rückenbreite (RB), Armlochdurchmesser (AD) und Brustbreite (BB) sowie Brustumfang (BU) Beachtung finden.

Die Zugaben richten sich nach dem jeweiligen Modell, dem verwendeten Material und den Tragevorlieben der Zielperson, allerdings kann man sich an folgenden Werten orientieren:

			Dress Robe Kleid	Waisted jacket Veste ajustée Taillierte Jacke	Loose jacket Veste seule Lose Jacke	Short length to full length coat Manteau court à manteau long Halbweiter Mantel bis Hängermantel
BAH	HD	RH	1 cm	1.5-2 cm	2-2.5 cm	3-3.5 cm
BAW	CD	RB	0.5 cm	1 cm	1-1.5 cm	1.5-2 cm
AD	DE	AD	1.5 cm	2 cm	2.5-3 cm	3-4 cm
BW	LP	BB	1.5 cm	1.5–2 cm	2 cm	2-2.5 cm
1/2 BC	1/2 TP	1/2 BU	3.5 cm	4.5–5 cm	5.5-6.5 cm	6.5-8.5 cm

Measurements slip

The measurements slip in the illustration, which can be used as a template, is used to compile all the measurements required to create the first pattern. In this way we can proceed with the assurance that we have not overlooked any measurements and there are no errors in our calculations.

Together with the measurements, other basic information can be added, such as the name of the customer or the date, and new entries, since the body obviously changes over time. "Observations on the figure" are better carried out on a regular basis and from a specific distance. Accurate observation at the beginning of the pattern-making process will make it much easier to take some decisions that need to be made later on. Some shapes and forms of the body can be drawn directly in the sketch for the basic pattern and in the design.

It is imperative to establish any deviations from the "normal body", even though no such "normal body" really exists. Standing in a stooped, crooked or very stiff position, shoulders at different heights, large shoulder blades, the depht and shape of the bust, the shape of the abdomen and hips, lordosis, large thighs, calves and knees, are some of the main characteristics that need to be taken into account. While creating the pattern (although also during the fitting stage), these specific characteristics should be checked and altered again and again.

A note should be made of the basic measurements at the top of the measurements slip: the body height (BH), bust circumference (BC), waist circumference (WAC), hip circumference (HC) and the individual hip

La fiche de mesures

La fiche de mesures de l'image, qui peut être utilisée comme modèle, sert à rassembler toutes les mesures nécessaires à la création du premier patron. C'est ainsi que nous pouvons procéder avec l'assurance de n'oublier aucune mesure et de les calculer toutes sans erreurs.

Nous pouvons ajouter aux mesures d'autres données essentielles comme, par exemple le nom de la cliente ou la date, de nouvelles entrées, puisque le corps va naturellement changer avec le temps. Il vaut mieux effectuer régulièrement les « observations de la silhouette » à une certaine distance. Une observation exacte au début de la création du patron facilite de nombreuses décisions à prendre plus tard. Dans l'ébauche du patron de base et dans le modèle, il est possible de dessiner directement certaines formes du corps.

Il est fondamental d'établir les écarts du « corps normal », même si ce « corps normal » n'existe pas réellement. Une position voutée, de côté ou très rigide, des hauteurs d'épaule différentes, de grosses omoplates, la hauteur et la forme de la poitrine, la forme de l'abdomen et des hanches, la lordose, les grosses cuisses, les muscles jumeaux et les genoux sont quelques unes des principales caractéristiques dont il faut tenir compte. Pendant la création du patron et même pendant l'essai, ces caractéristiques spécifiques doivent être vérifiées et modifiées à plusieurs reprises.

Dans la partie supérieure de la fiche de mesures les mesures de bases prises sont notées, c'est à dire la stature (S), le tour de poitrine (TP), le tour de taille (TT), le tour de hanches (TH) et la hauteur de cha-

Der Maßzettel

Der hier abgebildete Maßzettel, der als Kopiervorlage verwendet werden kann, dient der Erfassung aller für die Erstschnitterstellung erforderlichen Maße. So kann man sicher gehen, kein Maß zu vergessen und in der Maßberechnung fehlerlos vorzugehen.

Neben den Maßen sollte man auch weitere grundsätzliche Informationen, wie beispielsweise den Namen der Kundin oder das Datum, eintragen, denn der Körper unterliegt natürlich Veränderungen im Laufe der Zeit. Die „Figurbeobachtungen" werden am besten regelmäßig mit einem gewissen Abstand vorgenommen. Ein genaues Hinschauen zu Beginn der Schnitterstellung erleichtert so manche Entscheidung, die in späteren Etappen getroffen werden muss. In der Grundschnittskizze und der Figurine können die speziellen Körperformen direkt skizziert werden.

Besonders wichtig ist es, Abweichungen vom „Normkörper", den es natürlich nicht wirklich gibt, festzustellen. Eine gebückte, schiefe oder sehr aufrechte Haltung, ungleiche Schulterhöhe, starke Schulterblätter, die Höhe und Form der Brust, Bauch- und Hüftform, Hohlkreuz, gewölbte Schenkel, Waden oder Knie sind einige der wichtigsten Merkmale, die es festzuhalten gilt. Während der Schnitterstellung, aber auch bei der Anprobe sollten diese Besonderheiten immer wieder überprüft und überarbeitet werden.

Im oberen Teil des Maßzettels werden die gemessenen Grundmaße eingetragen, also die Körperhöhe (KH), der Brustumfang (BU), der Taillenumfang (TU), der Hüftumfang (HU) und die Individuelle Hüfttiefe,

Measurements Slip

Name:	Worked for:		Date:	
Observations on the figure:				
Posture:				

Standard size	measured	1/2	1/4	1/8
BH (Body height)				
BC (Bust circumference)				
WAC (Waist circumference)				
HC (Hip circumference)				
Individual hip depth (identifies the interval at the greatest point HC to WAC)				

Standard values	measured	balanced out	allowance	position
1/2 BNC (Base of the neck circumference)				
C (Collar)				
BAH (Back height)				
BL (Back length)				
HD (Hip depth)				
BD (Bust depth)				
FL (Front length)				
BAW (Back width)				
AD (Armhole diameter)				
BW (Bust width)				
1/2 BC (Bust circumference)				

Sleeve measurements	measured	formula/allowance	positioning
SW (Shoulder width)			
SL (Sleeve length)			
SHH (Sleeve head height)		BAH % 5 to 6 cm	
SLW (Sleeve width)		AD + allowance + 4.5 to 5.5 cm	
UAC (Upper arm circumference)		+ allowance 3 to 5 cm	
EC (Elbow circumference)			
WC (Wrist circumference)			
SHW (Sleeve hem width)			

La fiche de mesures

Nom:		Élaboré par:		Date:
Observations de la figure:				
Posture:				

Taille normalisée	mesurée	1/2	1/4	1/8
S (Stature)				
TP (Tour de poitrine)				
TT (Tour de taille)				
TH (Tour de hanches)				
Longueur taille-bassin individuelle (définit la distance entre les points les plus marqués de TH à TT)				

Valeurs normalisées	mesurée	compensée	ajout	montée
1/2 TC (Encolure)				
C (C)				
HD (Hauteur du dos)				
LD (Longueur du dos)				
LTB (Longueur taille-bassin)				
PP (Profondeur de poitrine)				
LDe (Longueur de devant)				
CD (carrure dos)				
DE (Diamètre d'emmanchure)				
LP (Largeur de poitrine)				
1/2 TP (Tour de poitrine)				

Mesures des manches	mesurées	formule/ajout		montées
LE (Longueur d'épaule)				
LoM (Longueur de manche)				
HTM (Hauteur de tête de manche)		HD % 5 à 6 cm		
LaM (Largeur de manche)		DE + ajout + 4,5 à 5,5 cm		
TBP (Tour de bras plié)		+ ajout 3 à 5 cm		
TCo (Tour de coude)				
TPo (Tour de poignet)				
LBM (Largeur de bord de manche)				

Maßzettel

Name:		Gearbeitet für:	Datum:	
Figurbeobachtungen:				
Haltung:				

Normgröße	gemessen	1/2	1/4	1/8
KH (Körperhöhe)				
BU (Brustumfang)				
TU (Taillenumfang)				
HU (Hüftumfang)				
Individuelle Hüfttiefe (bezeichnet den Abstand der stärksten Stelle HU zu TU)				

Normwerte	gemessen	ausgeglichen	Zugabe	aufstellen
1/2 HSU (Halsansatzumfang)				
HS (Halsspiegel)				
RH (Rückenhöhe)				
RL (Rückenlänge)				
HT (Hüfttiefe)				
BT (Brusttiefe)				
VL (Vorderlänge)				
RB (Rückenbreite)				
AD (Armlochdurchmesser)				
BB (Brustbreite)				
1/2 BU (Brustumfang)				

Ärmelmaße	gemessen	Formel/Zugabe	aufstellen
SCHB (Schulterbreite)			
ÄLG (Ärmellänge)			
ÄKH (Ärmelkugelhöhe)		RH % 5 bis 6 cm	
ÄB (Ärmelbreite)		AD + Zugabe + 4,5 bis 5,5 cm	
OAU (Oberarmumfang)		+ Zugabe 3 bis 5 cm	
ELLBU (Ellbogenumfang)			
HGU (Handgelenkumfang)			
ÄSW (Ärmelsaumweite)			

height, that is to say, the vertical distance from the hip to the waist, and the shoulder width (SW). Using halves, quarters and eighths of these measurements will speed up the pattern-making process later on.

The following values should be checked in the measuring chart or calculated using formulas. If in doubt, as a beginner it is better to use the calculated measurements for guidance. The data is entered, and the final sum added up and calculated.

The sleeve length (SL), the upper arm circumference (UAC) and the sleeve hem width (SHW) are measured and made a note of. The height of the sleeve head height (SHH) and the sleeve width (SLW) are calculated with the help of the corresponding formulas.

Once the measurements slip has been completed, we can start on the specific work for making up the basic patterns.

In the following pages we shall offer step-by-step explanations for making basic patterns for skirts, dresses and fitted garments. This can be used as a basic system for the creative configuration of models and can be applied to any set of measurements. The examples of models obtained give us a general idea of the unlimited range of possibilities for configuring patterns, and show us some basic techniques, such as how to proceed with darts, the creation of silhouettes and pleating, for example.

que hanche, c'est à dire la distance verticale de la hanche à la taille, et la largeur d'épaule (LE). Grâce aux moitiés, quarts et huitièmes de ces mesures, une procédure plus rapide au cours de la création ultérieure du dessin de patron est possible.

Ce qui suit sont les valeurs qui doivent nous renvoyer au tableau de mesures ou qui se calculent avec des formules. En cas de doute, en tant que débutant, il vaut mieux tenir compte des mesures calculées. Les données sont saisies, additionnées et le total final est calculé.

La longueur de manche (LoM), le tour de bras plié (TBP) et la largeur de bord de manche (LBM) se mesurent et sont notées. La hauteur de tête de manche (HTM) et la largeur de manche (LaM) se calculent à l'aide des formules correspondantes.

Une fois la fiche de mesures entièrement complétée, nous pouvons commencer le travail concret dans les patrons de base.

Nous allons expliquer étape par étape dans les pages suivantes comment créer des patrons de base pour des jupes, des robes et des vêtements ajustés. Le tout servira de système de base pour la configuration créative de modèles et peut s'appliquer à tout ensemble de mesures. Les exemples de modèles qui en résultent nous proposent une vision générale des possibilités illimitées de variation de la configuration des patrons et nous transmettent des techniques de base comme, par exemple, la manière de procéder avec les pinces, la création de silhouettes et le plissé.

also der vertikal gemessene Abstand des Hüftrings zur Taille, und die Schulterbreite (SCHB). Die halbierten, gevierteIten und geachtelten Maße ermöglichen es, bei der späteren Aufstellung der Schnittzeichnung schneller vorgehen zu können.

Dann folgen die Werte, bei deren Entwicklung man die Maßtabelle zum Vergleich heranzieht oder die man an Hand von Formeln errechnet. Im Zweifelsfall sollte man sich als Anfänger eher auf die berechneten Maße stützen. Die Zugaben werden ebenfalls eingetragen, addiert und die Endsumme ermittelt.

Ärmellänge (ÄLG), Oberarmumfang (OAU) und die gewünschte Ärmelsaumweite (ÄSW) werden gemessen und eingetragen. Die Ärmelkugelhöhe (ÄKH) und die Ärmelbreite (ÄB) werden dagegen mit Hilfe der entsprechenden Formeln ermittelt.

Wenn der Maßzettel vollständig ausgefüllt ist, kann die konkrete Arbeit an den Grundschnitten beginnen.

Auf den folgenden Seiten werden die Grundschnittkonstruktionen für den Rock und das Kleid bzw. enge Kleidungsstücke Schritt für Schritt erklärt. Sie dienen als Basis-System für die kreative Modellgestaltung und können auf jedes individuelle Maß-Set angewandt werden. Die darauf folgenden Modellbeispiele geben einen Ausblick auf die schier unbegrenzten Variationsmöglichkeiten der Schnittgestaltung und vermitteln einige grundlegende Techniken, wie zum Beispiel den Umgang mit Abnähern, das Kreieren von Silhouetten und das Faltenlegen.

	Measurement Nom de la mensuration Maßbezeichnung	Measurments in cm Dimensions en cm Maße in cm						
S T GR	Size Taille Größe	6/8 36 34	8/10 38 36	10/12 40 38	12/14 42 40	14/16 44 42	16/18 46 44	18/20 48 46
BH S KH	Body height Stature Körperhöhe	168	168	168	168	168	168	168
BC TP BU	Bust circumference Tour de poitrine Brustumfang	80	80	88	92	96	96	104
WAC TT TU	Waist circumference Tour de taille Taillenumfang	64	68	72	76	80	84	88
HC TH HU	Hip circumference Tour de hanches Hüftumfang	91	94	97	100	103	106	109
BNC TC HSU	Base of the neckline circumference Encolure Halsansatzumfang	34.8	35.4	36	36.6	37.2	37.8	38.4
C C HS	Collar Col Halsspiegel	6.5	6.6	6.7	6.8	6.9	7	7.1
BAH HD RH	Back height Hauteur du dos Rückenhöhe	19.3	19.7	20.1	20.5	20.9	21.3	21.7
BL LD RL	Back length Longueur du dos Rückenlänge	41.2	41.4	41.6	41.8	42	42.2	42.4
HD LTB HT	Hip depth Longueur taille-bassin Hüfttiefe	61.4	61.8	62.2	62.6	63	63.4	63.8
BD PP BT	Bust depth Profondeur de poitrine Brusttiefe	26.5	27.3	28.1	28.9	29.7	30.5	31.3
FL LDe VL	Front length Longueur de devant Vorderlänge	44.1	44.7	45.3	45.9	46.5	47.1	47.7
BAW CD RB	Back width Carrure dos Rückenbreite	15.5	16	16.5	17	17.5	18	18.5
AD DE AD	Armhole diameter Diamètre d'emmanchure Armlochdurchmesser	7.9	8.6	9.3	10	10.7	11.4	12.1
BW LP BB	Bust width Largeur de poitrine Brustbreite	16.6	17.4	18.2	19	19.8	20.6	21.4
SW LE SCHB	Shoulder width Longueur d'épaule Schulterbreite	11.8	12	12.2	12.4	12.6	12.8	13
SL LoM ÄLG	Sleeve length Longueur de manche Ärmellänge	59.3	59.6	59.9	60.2	60.5	60.8	61.1
UAC TBP OAU	Upper arm circumference Tour de bras plié Oberarmumfang	25.6	26.8	28	29.2	30.4	21.6	32.8
WC Tpo HGU	Wrist circumference Tour de poignet Handgelenkumfang	15	15.4	15.8	16.2	16.6	17	17.4
ABC APP WBA	Angle of bust dart Angle de pince de poitrine Winkel Brustabnäher	11.5°	13°	14.5°	16°	17.5°	19°	20.5°

The basic pattern for a straight skirt
Patron de base pour jupe droite
Der gerade Rockgrundschnitt

The measured sample measurements:
WAC Waist circumference 68 cm – 34 cm
HC Hip circumference 98 cm – 49 cm
HD Hip depth 20 cm
SKL Skirt length 60 cm

The calculated sample measurements:
1/2 WAC Waist circumference (34 cm) + *1 cm width allowance* = 35 cm
1/2 HC Hip circumference (49 cm) + *1 cm width allowance* = 50 cm
The slack (difference between HC and WAC) = 15 cm
Slack distribution: side seam: 7 cm, front part: 2.5 cm, back part: 5.5 cm

Dimensions de modèle mesurées :
TT Tour de taille 68 cm - 34 cm
TH Tour de hanches 98 cm - 49 cm
LTB Longueur taille-bassin 20 cm
LJ Longueur de jupe 60 cm

Dimensions de modèle calculées :
1/2 TT Tour de taille (34 cm) + *1 cm de plus en largeur* = 35 cm
1/2 TH Tour de hanches (49 cm) + *1 cm supplémentaire en largeur* = 50 cm
Le retrait (écart entre TH et TT) = 15 cm
Distribution du retrait : Couture latérale : 7 cm, partie avant : 2,5 cm, partie arrière : 5,5 cm

Die gemessenen Beispielmaße:
TU Taillenumfang 68 cm – 34 cm
HU Hüftumfang 98 cm – 49 cm
HT Hüfttiefe 20 cm
ROL Rocklänge 60 cm

Die berechneten Beispielmaße:
1/2 TU Taillenumfang (34 cm) + *1 cm Weitenzugabe* = 35 cm
1/2 HU Hüftumfang (49 cm) + *1 cm Weitenzugabe* = 50 cm
Der Ausfall (Differenz zwischen HU und TU) = 15 cm
Die Ausfallverteilung: Seitennaht: 7 cm, Vorderteil: 2,5 cm, Rückenteil: 5,5 cm

The basic pattern for a straight skirt serves as the basis for most skirt patterns. It is always positioned straight and based on the waist. In this way the perfect fit can best be worked out and all alterations are dealt with without problem in a calculated ratio. The skirt pattern is fitted to the body, beginning with the widest point of the body for compiling the basic pattern – the hip circumference. The waist circumference, narrower in comparison to the hips, is achieved by using darts in the waist. The difference between the waist and hip circumference is also slack. Depending on the shape of the body and the skirt pattern, the distribution of slack on the front and back parts is varied and must often be fitted when trying on.

Le patron de base pour jupe droite sert de support à la plupart des modèles de jupe. Il est toujours élaboré en ligne droite à partir de la taille. Le vêtement s'adapte ainsi parfaitement et toutes les retouches peuvent être réalisées sans problème dans des proportions calculées. Le modèle de jupe s'ajuste au corps et le patron de base est défini en partant de la mensuration la plus large du corps : le tour de hanches. Le tour de taille, plus petit que celui des hanches, est obtenu à partir de réductions au niveau de la taille. L'écart entre le tour de taille et celui des hanches est appelé le retrait. En fonction de la forme du corps et du modèle de jupe, le retrait se répartit différemment sur la partie avant et arrière, et doit souvent est ajusté pendant l'essayage.

Der gerade Rockgrundschnitt dient als Grundlage für die meisten Rockmodelle. Er wird immer gerade und von der Taille ausgehend aufgestellt. Dadurch lässt sich die perfekte Passform am besten herausarbeiten und alle Änderungen lassen sich problemlos in einem rechnerischen Verhältnis vornehmen. Das Rockmodell wird dem Körper angepasst, indem man bei der Grundschnittaufstellung mit der breitesten Stelle des Körpers – dem Hüftumfang – beginnt. Der im Vergleich zur Hüfte schmalere Taillenumfang wird mit Hilfe von Abnehmern in der Taille erreicht. Die Differenz zwischen Taille und Hüftumfang bezeichnet man auch als Ausfall. Je nach Körperform und Rockmodell variiert die Ausfallverteilung auf das Vorder- und Rückenteil und muss oft noch bei der Anprobe angepasst werden.

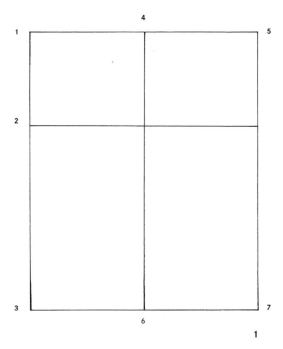

1. 1 - 2: You begin the basic pattern at the centre front, defining Point 1. You attain Point 2 through a vertical line of 20 cm (the hip depth) which is drawn downwards from this point.

1 - 3: Following this line, you cut down the skirt length (60 cm) starting at Point 1 and going to Point 3. Later, this length can be optionally shortened or lengthened. From all three points (1, 2 and 3) lines at a right angle are drawn to the right.

1 - 5: Then the waistline (half hip circumference with 49 cm + *1 cm width allowance*) is cut away from Point 1. Point 5 is formed.

5 - 7: To find the line at the centre back, you cut down the skirt length from Point 5 again. Along this line, the pattern is later put up against the centre fold of the fabric.

4 - 6: You obtain the reference for the side seam by halving the length from 1-5. You then go out from Point 1 for the distance of this measurement and in this way Point 4 is formed. Point 6 is made by going along the same amount at Point 3. Afterwards, both points (4 and 6) are linked to each other.

The left rectangle made in this way forms the front part and the adjacent right area is the back part of the pattern.

1. 1 - 2: Le patron de base est entamé en définissant le point 1 sur le milieu du dos. Le point 2 est obtenu en traçant une ligne verticale de 20 cm (longueur taille-bassin) vers le bas.

1 - 3: En partant de cette ligne au point 1, la longueur de la jupe (60 cm) est tracée et permet d'obtenir le point 3. Cette longueur peut être ensuite raccourcie ou allongée selon les besoins. À partir de ces trois points (1, 2 et 3), des lignes sont tracées en angle droit vers la droite.

1 - 5: La ligne de la taille est ensuite tirée (demi-tour de hanches avec 49 cm + *1 cm supplémentaire en largeur*) à partir du point 1. Le point 5 est alors créé.

5 - 7: Afin d'obtenir la ligne de le milieu du dos, la longueur de la jupe est à nouveau tracée à partir du point 5. Le patron est par la suite placé sur cette ligne au niveau de la coupe du tissu.

4 - 6: La référence de la couture latérale s'obtient en divisant par deux le segment 1 - 5. Cette mesure est appliquée à partir du point 1 pour créer le point 4. Le point 6 est obtenu en reportant la même valeur à partir du point 3. Les deux points (4 et 6) sont ensuite reliés.

Le rectangle gauche constitue la partie avant et la surface située à sa droite, la partie arrière du modèle.

1. 1 - 2: Den Grundschnitt beginnt man an der Vorderen Mitte, indem man den Punkt 1 definiert. Punkt 2 erhält man durch eine senkrechte Linie von 20 cm (die Hüfttiefe), die von diesem Punkt nach unten gezogen wird.

1 - 3: Auf dieser Linie trägt man vom Punkt 1 ausgehend die Rocklänge (60 cm) ab und erhält dadurch Punkt 3. Diese Länge ist später beliebig kürz- oder verlängerbar. Von allen drei Punkten (1, 2 und 3) werden Linien im rechten Winkel nach rechts gezogen.

1 - 5: Dann wird die Taillenlinie (halber Hüftumfang mit 49 cm + *1 cm Weitenzugabe*) von Punkt 1 abgetragen. Es entsteht Punkt 5.

5 - 7: Um die Linie der Hinteren Mitte zu erhalten, trägt man von Punkt 5 erneut die Rocklänge ab. An dieser Linie wird später der Schnitt an den Stoffbruch angelegt.

4 - 6: Die Referenz für die Seitennaht erhält man, indem man die Strecke 1 – 5 halbiert. Dieses Maß wird dann im Punkt 1 abgetragen, und so entsteht Punkt 4. Punkt 6 ergibt sich, indem man denselben Wert im Punkt 3 abträgt. Danach werden beide Punkte (4 und 6) miteinander verbunden.

Das so entstandene linke Rechteck bildet das Vorderteil, und der anliegende rechte Bereich ist das Rückenteil des Modells.

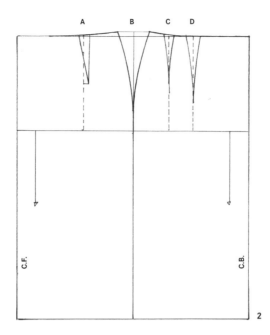

A   B   C   D

C.F.

C.B.

2

2. Now the slack on the waistline is cut away to fit the skirt to the shape of the body. Following the calculation for the slack, a total of 7 cm on the side seam is taken out, on the front part 2.5 cm and the back part 5.5 cm. In the case of the back part, one dart is sufficient up to a dart size of 3 to 4 cm, in the case of a larger amount of slack, the quantity is distributed between two darts as in the example shown here. To draw in the appropriate darts, you proceed as follows:

At dart A (*at an interval of 6 to 8 cm to the side seam*) a total of 2.5 cm is taken out. *The length* should amount to *9 to 11 cm*. It is recommended that you lay the points of the darts at *1 cm to the right* to achieve an optimal fit.

7 cm are taken out at the side seam B, i.e. 3.5 cm per side. Depending on the curve of the body, the side seam curve is then marked out coming back again into the straight side seam at the latest at hip height (line 2).

Dart D is located at half length between the side seam and the break line; 3 cm width and *14 to 15 cm length* is taken out with this.

Dart C with 2.5 cm width and a *length of 12 to 13 cm* is exactly between the side seam and dart D.

2. Afin d'ajuster la jupe à la forme du corps, le retrait est calculé au niveau de la ligne de la taille. D'après le calcul du retrait, 7 cm au total sont supprimés de la couture latérale, 2,5 cm de la partie avant et 5,5 cm de la partie arrière. Une pince de 3 à 4 cm au maximum est suffisante sur la partie arrière ; si le retrait est supérieur, la totalité est distribuée sur deux pinces, tel que l'illustre l'exemple suivant. Pour dessiner la pince correspondante, suivez les étapes suivantes :

Au total, 2,5 cm correspondent à la pince A (*à une distance de 6 à 8 cm de la couture latérale*). *La longueur* doit être de *9 à 11 cm*. Il est recommandé de plier l'extrémité de la pince *1 cm à droite* , pour obtenir une assise optimale.

7 cm correspondent à la couture latérale B, soit 3,5 cm de chaque côté. La courbe de la couture latérale est tracée en fonction de la courbe du corps, qui recoupe finalement à nouveau la couture latérale droite à hauteur des hanches (ligne 2).

La pince D se trouve à égale distance entre la couture latérale et la ligne de coupe; ici 3 cm sont supprimés en largeur *14 à 15 cm en longueur* .

La pince C se trouve exactement entre la couture latérale et la pince D, avec une largeur de 2,5 cm et une *longueur de 12 à 13 cm*.

2. Nun wird der Ausfall an der Taillenlinie abgetragen, um den Rock der Körperform anzuformen. Der Ausfallberechnung folgend, entfallen auf die Seitennaht insgesamt 7 cm, auf das Vorderteil 2,5 cm und das Rückenteil 5,5 cm. Beim Rückenteil ist bis zu einer Abnähergröße von 3 bis 4 cm ein Abnäher ausreichend, bei einem größeren Ausfall wird der Betrag auf zwei Abnäher verteilt wie in dem hier gezeigten Beispiel. Um die entsprechenden Abnäher einzuzeichnen, geht man wie folgt vor:

Auf Abnäher A (*im Abstand von 6 bis 8 cm zur Seitennaht*) entfallen insgesamt 2,5 cm. *Die Länge* sollte *9 bis 11 cm* betragen. Es empfiehlt sich, die Abnäherspitze um *1 cm nach rechts* zu verlegen, um einen optimalen Sitz zu erreichen.

Auf die Seitennaht B entfallen 7 cm, also 3,5 cm pro Seite. Je nach Körperrundung wird dann der Seitennahtbogen ausgezeichnet, der spätestens in Hüfthöhe (Linie 2) wieder in die gerade Seitennaht einläuft.

Der Abnäher D befindet sich auf halber Strecke zwischen der Seitennaht und der Bruchlinie; auf ihn entfallen 3 cm Breite und *14 bis 15 cm Länge* .

Genau zwischen Seitennaht und Abnäher D liegt der Abnäher C mit 2,5 cm Breite und einer *Länge von 12 bis 13 cm*.

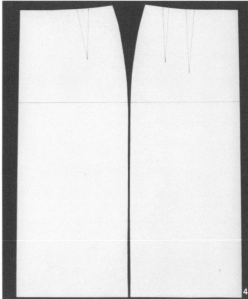

The basic line on the side seam is *increased by 1 cm* to follow the curve of the body. On the next horizontal darts (A and C), yet more *0.5 cm* is taken out. Now the waistline is drawn in a rounded form. The darts in the back part of the skirt (C and D) should be slightly drawn on a convex.

3. The curve of the hip on the side seam is marked with the curve ruler and depending on the shape of the body runs in again at the latest at the hipline along the straight side seam. This curve must often be fitted when trying on.

4. Now the two parts of the skirt – that is the centre front and centre back – are copied out and the hipline and darts drawn in exactly. The number and shape of the darts vary depending on the shape of the body and are often individually fitted when trying on. In this way, for example, it may be necessary to insert two darts on the front part if the woman has a rounded stomach.

La ligne de base sur la couture latérale *augmente de 1 cm* pour s'ajuster à la courbe du corps. Sur les deux pinces suivantes (A et C), *0,5 cm* sont également supprimés. La ligne de la taille est ensuite tracée en forme circulaire. Le tracé des pinces de la partie arrière de la jupe (C et D) doit être légèrement convexe.

3. La courbe des hanches sur la couture latérale doit être dessinée avec la règle à tracer les courbes et, selon la forme du corps, celle-ci recoupe finalement la ligne des hanches au niveau de la couture latérale droite. Cette courbe doit être fréquemment ajustée lors de l'essayage.

4. Les deux milieus de la jupe (avant et arrière) sont ensuite copiées et la ligne des hanches, ainsi que les pinces, sont méticuleusement dessinées. Le nombre et la forme des pinces varient en fonction de la forme du corps et doivent souvent être adaptés lors de l'essayage suivant chaque cas individuel. Par exemple, si la femme a le ventre rond, il peut s'avérer nécessaire de réaliser deux pinces sur la partie avant.

Die Grundlinie an der Seitennaht wird *1 cm erhöht*, um der Körperrundung zu folgen. Auf die nächst liegenden Abnäher (A und C) entfallen noch weitere *0,5 cm*. Nun wird die Taillenlinie gerundet eingezeichnet. Die Abnäher im hinteren Rockteil (C und D) sollten leicht konvex gezeichnet werden.

3. Die Hüftrundung an der Seitennaht wird mit dem Kurvenlineal eingezeichnet und läuft je nach Körperform spätestens an der Hüftlinie wieder in die gerade Seitennaht ein. Diese Rundung muss oft noch bei der Anprobe angepasst werden.

4. Nun werden die zwei Rockteile – die Vordere und Hintere Mitte – herauskopiert und Hüftlinie und Abnäher genau eingezeichnet. Anzahl und Form der Abnäher variieren je nach Körperform und werden oft noch bei der Anprobe individuell angepasst. So kann es beispielsweise bei einem stärkeren Bauchansatz nötig werden, am Vorderteil zwei Abnäher einzulegen.

5. At the first fitting you must ensure that the side seams always run straight along the side of the body. Furthermore, the darts are checked and if necessary moved or even additional darts added.

5. Lors du premier essayage, il faut veiller à ce que les coutures latérales restent toujours sur les côtés du corps. Pour finir, il convient de vérifier les pinces et, si nécessaire, de les réduire ou d'en ajouter de nouvelles.

5. Bei der ersten Anprobe ist darauf zu achten, dass die Seitennähte immer gerade entlang der Körperseite verlaufen. Des Weiteren werden die Abnäher überprüft und gegebenenfalls verlegt bzw. zusätzliche Abnäher hinzugefügt.

Slightly flared skirt with folds lying over each other
Jupe exposée de manière simple avec des plis superposés
Leicht ausgestellter Rock mit übereinander liegenden Falten

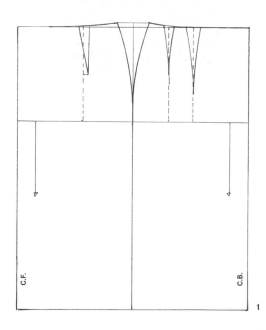

C.F.

C.B.

1

1. An almost endless number of variations can be developed from a basic skirt pattern. This one here has two overlapping folds in the front part and a slightly flared outline. It is therefore suitable for a fabric with a certain class and a changeable shine. Because of the asymmetrical front we are drawing the front part in its full width.

1. À partir du patron de base de la jupe, il est possible d'obtenir une infinité de variantes. Celle que nous voyons ici possède deux plis superposés sur la partie avant et dessine légèrement la silhouette. Le tissu approprié pour confectionner celle-ci devrait présenter une certaine texture et un brillant irisé. Étant donné sa partie avant asymétrique, il faut dessiner celle-ci avec toute sa largeur.

1. Aus dem Rockgrundschnitt kann eine schier endlose Zahl an Variationen entwickelt werden. Diese hier hat im Vorderteil zwei sich überlappende Falten und eine leicht ausgestellte Silhouette. Dafür eignet sich ein Stoff mit einem gewissen Stand und einem changierenden Glanz. Wegen der asymmetrischen Front zeichnen wir das Vorderteil in seiner ganzen Breite.

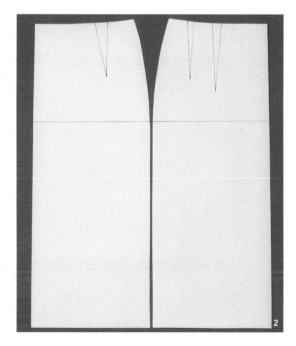

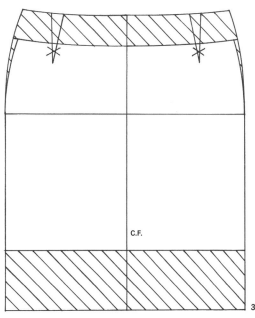

C.F.

2-3. Since the basic pattern reaches from the waist to the knee, for this pattern it is shortened 12 cm at the hem. The waistband also slips 6 cm down. The sketch here shows the opened front part with the front centre front in the middle. Because of the reduction caused by the band the darts are tapered into even smaller points which are not sewn for visual reasons. The remaining dart width of approx. 1 cm on the decreased waistline is taken way at the side seam. At the back part, you proceed in the same way; the waistline is decreased and minimized around a dart width at the side seam.

2-3. Étant donné que le patron de base va de la taille jusqu'au genou, l'ourlet sera raccourci de 12 cm sur ce modèle. De plus, la fermeture au niveau de la taille sera rabaissée de 6 cm. Le croquis indiqué ici montre la partie avant pliée avec le milieu avant placée au centre. En rabaissant l'ensemble, les pinces sont réduites à de légères ondulations qui ne seront pas cousues pour des raisons esthétiques. Avec la ligne de la taille plus basse, la largeur de la pince restante est d'environ 1 cm et sera reprise sur les coutures latérales. Dans le dos, la procédure est semblable, la ligne de la taille est rabaissée et la largeur de pince est réduite au niveau des coutures latérales.

2-3. Da der Grundschnitt von der Taille bis zum Knie hinunter reicht, wird er für dieses Modell 12 cm am Saum gekürzt. Der Taillenbund rutscht zudem um 6 cm nach unten. Die Skizze hier zeigt das aufgeklappte Vorderteil mit der Vorderen Mitte im Zentrum. Durch das Herabsetzen des Bundes sind die Abnäher auf nur noch kleine Spitzen reduziert, die aus optischen Gründen nicht genäht werden. Die verbleibende Abnäherbreite an der herabgesetzten Taillenlinie von ca. 1 cm wird an der Seitennaht weggenommen. Am Rückenteil geht man entsprechend vor; die Taillenlinie wird herabgesetzt und um die Abnäherbreite an der Seitennaht verringert.

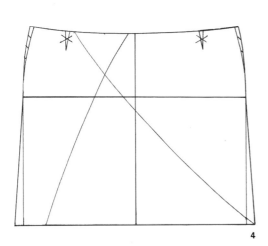

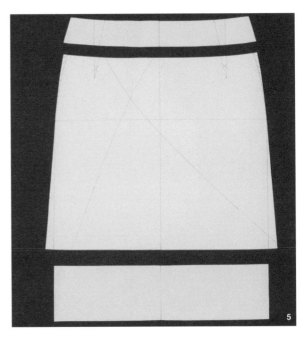

4

5

4-5. To obtain a slightly flared outline, the side seam is extended by 2 cm at the hem. The new side line formed in this way runs at waist height into the original side seam. This modification is also undertaken on the back part. On the front part, the position of the folds is established and drawn in with a slightly rounded line. The position and form of the folds is decided according to the individual design.

6. When overlapping the two folds, it is important to ensure that the fold depth of the upper fold is large enough for the lower one to lie flat underneath. The cut front part, as you can see here, displays the flat skirt. The additional volume, which is necessary in the fabric for the folding, must now be worked in to the cut. For this the two side parts are copied, and indeed in each case from the side seam up to the drawn in, intersecting fold line. Afterwards the copied parts are cut out

4-5. Afin de pouvoir exposer une silhouette simple, l'ourlet est rallongé de 2 cm au niveau des coutures latérales. La couture latérale ainsi obtenue arrive à hauteur des hanches de la couture latérale d'origine. Cette retouche est également effectuée dans le dos. Sur la partie avant, la position des plis sera établie en suivant une ligne légèrement courbe. La position et la forme des plis dépendront de chaque modèle.

6. En superposant les deux plis, il est important que la profondeur du pli supérieur soit suffisamment importante pour que le pli inférieur reste plat en dessous. La partie avant de la coupe, telle qu'elle est présentée ici, montre la jupe plissée. Le volume supplémentaire nécessaire sur le tissu pour créer les plis devra maintenant être ajouté au moment de la coupe. Deux pièces latérales seront pour cela jointes, allant de la couture latérale jusqu'aux lignes tracées et entrecroisées des plis.

4-5. Um eine leicht ausgestellte Silhouette zu erreichen, wird die Seitennaht am Saum um 2 cm erweitert. Die so entstandene neue Seitenlinie läuft auf Hüfthöhe in die ursprüngliche Seitennaht ein. Diese Modifikation wird auch am Rückenteil vorgenommen. Am Vorderteil wird die Lage der Falten festgelegt und mit einer leicht gerundeten Linie eingezeichnet. Die Position und Form der Falten wird je nach Design gestaltet.

6. Bei der Überlappung der beiden Falten ist es wichtig darauf zu achten, dass die Faltentiefe der oberen Falte so groß ist, dass die untere glatt darunter liegt. Das Schnittvorderteil, so wie man es hier sieht, stellt den glatten Rock dar. Das zusätzliche Volumen, das im Stoff für die Falten benötigt wird, muss jetzt in den Schnitt eingearbeitet werden. Dazu werden die zwei seitlichen Teile abkopiert, und zwar jeweils von der Seitennaht bis hin zur eingezeich-

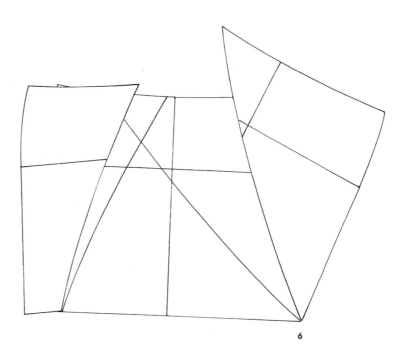

6

and the original front part of the skirt remains without alterations. The cut out extra parts are now laid on the original part with the points touching in the area of the hem. In the waist area, the interval between should amount to the width of the fold which has been freely fixed. Then the side parts are stuck down.

7. In the next step, the paper is folded according to the layout of the line of folds, preferably over a table edge. The folds are added in the same way as they are afterwards with the fabric. The curve of the fold lines is not easy to be fixed since paper is fundamentally more unwieldy than fabric. This extra effort is however worth it, since slight curves give a nice drape and are visually more attractive. Alternatively the lines can also of course be drawn straight, vertically or diagonally from the waist to the hem. If you now level out the waistline, i.e. if you cut it straight, there is a jagged

Pour finir, les pièces copiées sont découpées en laissant intacte la partie avant d'origine de la jupe. Les pièces supplémentaires découpées seront mises en place sur la pièce de coupe de sortie de sorte que les extrémités se touchent dans la zone de l'ourlet. Au niveau de la taille, la distance de la position équivaut à la largeur des plis fixés de manière aléatoire. Les pièces latérales seront alors jointes.

7. L'étape suivante consistera à plier le papier (si possible en utilisant le rebord d'une table) en suivant la ligne des plis. Les plis seront disposés dans la position définitive qu'ils adopteront sur le tissu. Il n'est pas évident d'établir la courbure des lignes de pli, étant donné que le papier s'avère moins maniable que le tissu. Cependant, ces dépenses supplémentaires valent la peine, puisqu'une légère courbure donne un effet de pli plus joli et attire davantage l'attention visuellement. Il est

neten, sich überschneidenden Faltenlinie. Anschließend werden die kopierten Teile ausgeschnitten, das ursprüngliche Rockvorderteil bleibt ohne Veränderungen bestehen. Die ausgeschnittenen Extra-Teile werden nun auf das Ausgangsschnittteil gelegt, wobei sich die Spitzen im Saumbereich berühren sollen. Im Taillenbereich beträgt der Anlegeabstand die Breite des frei festgelegten Falteninhalts. Dann werden die Seitenteile festgeklebt.

7. Im nächsten Schritt wird das Papier, am besten über einer Tischkante, gemäß der Linienführung der Falten geknickt. Die Falten werden so zugelegt, wie es nachher beim Stoff der Fall sein wird. Die Rundung der Faltenlinien ist nicht so leicht fixierbar, da Papier wesentlich unhandlicher ist als Stoff. Dieser Mehraufwand lohnt sich allerdings, da leichte Rundungen einen schönen Faltenwurf ergeben und optisch ansprechender sind. Alternativ können die

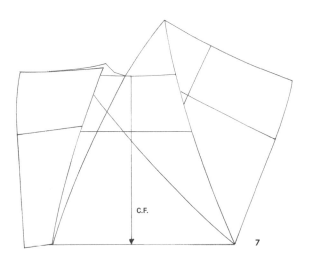

C.F.

7

8

waistline when you open out the pattern part again. That is exactly the fold content that the folds need when they are added.

8. It is helpful to mark the position and shape of the folds on the fabric with chalk or thread stitches.
In this way, the fabric can be shaped by hand and possibly be fixed by ironing.

bien sûr possible de réaliser des lignes droites, verticales ou en diagonale de la taille jusqu'à l'ourlet. Si la ligne de la taille est nivelée, c'est-à-dire si elle est coupée droite, cela produira alors un effet dentelé au niveau de la taille en dépliant à nouveau les pièces de coupe. Cela correspond exactement au contenu des plis, nécessaire à ceux-ci au moment de se déplier.

8. Il s'avère utile d'effectuer des repères sur le tissu pour indiquer l'emplacement et la forme des plis à l'aide d'une craie ou par points de couture.
Il est ainsi possible de donner une forme au tissu avec les mains et de la maintenir avec le fer à repasser.

Linien natürlich auch gerade, senkrecht oder diagonal von der Taille zum Saum gezogen werden. Gleicht man nun die Taillenlinie aus, d.h. schneidet man sie gerade, ergibt sich beim erneuten Aufklappen des Schnittteils ein zackiger Taillenausschnitt. Das ist exakt der Falteninhalt, den die Falten beim Zulegen brauchen.

8. Es ist hilfreich, Lage und Form der Falten mit Kreide oder Fadenstichen auf dem Stoff zu markieren.
So kann der Stoff dann von Hand geformt und evtl. durch Bügeln fixiert werden.

Asymmetrical balloon skirt with slanting pockets and round yoke
Jupe ballon asymétrique à poches obliques et ceinture corset arrondie
Asymmetrischer Ballonrock mit schrägen Eingriffstaschen und runder Passe

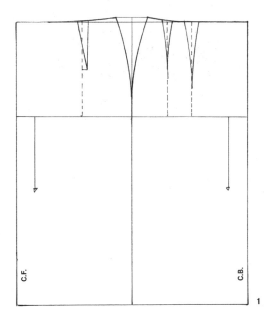

C.F.

C.B.

1

1. With this variant of the straight skirt pattern, you work with the so-called fanning out cut by cutting into the paper cut-out and opening up the diverse pattern parts. In this way, you achieve additional volume which is then placed on the body through sequencing or interlacing of folds.

1. Pour cette variante de coupe droite d'une jupe, nous utilisons les dénommées fermetures de coupe, qui consistent à couper les bouts de papier et à faire pivoter les différentes pièces de coupe. Nous obtenons ainsi un volume supplémentaire, qui est ensuite ajusté au corps avec des coutures ou des plis.

1. Bei dieser Variante des geraden Rockschnittes arbeitet man mit der sogenannten Schnittaufsperrung, indem man in den Papierschnitt hinein schneidet und die diversen Schnittteile aufdreht. Auf diese Weise erhält man zusätzliches Volumen, das dann durch Einreihen oder Faltenlegung am Körper platziert wird.

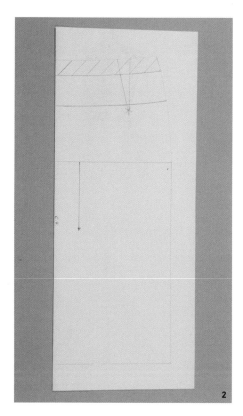

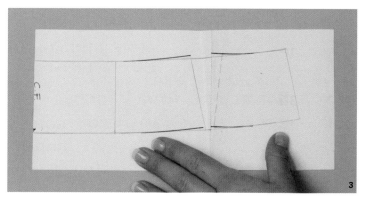

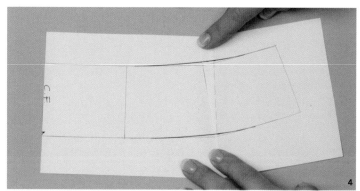

2. If you do not want the skirt to sit right on the waist, you go downwards from the basic pattern approx. 4 to 6 cm. At this new waistline you then cut away the desired width – in this case 6 cm – for the belt-shaped yoke.

3-4. The dart of the basic pattern must be added in the paper cut-out, the dart content being removed to adjust the yoke to the round waist shape and at the same time avoid unattractive dart seams. To achieve this, the paper is folded on the dart lines and laid on itself, so then the yoke becomes round and the cut edges correspond. It is important to ensure that a right angle is maintained at all corners of the outside edge, both at the centre back and also at the centre front and the side seam.

2 . Si vous ne souhaitez pas ajuster la jupe à la taille, celle-ci peut être rabaissée entre 4 et 6 cm à partir de la coupe de base. Puis, la largeur désirée est nivelée par rapport à la nouvelle ligne de la taille —dans ce cas 6 cm— pour la ceinture corset en forme de ceinture.

3-4. La pince du modèle de base doit être ajoutée au patron en papier, de sorte que le volume des pinces puisse être éliminé afin d'adapter la ceinture corset à la forme arrondie de la taille, tout en évitant d'avoir à coudre des pinces inesthétiques. Le papier devra pour cela être plié suivant les lignes des pinces et sera superposé, de sorte que la ceinture corset s'arrondisse et, de manière identique, les bords de coupe soient équilibrés. Il est important de veiller à maintenir un angle droit au niveau de tous les angles du bord extérieur, ainsi que de la partie arrière, de la partie centrale avant et sur le côté.

2. Will man den Rock nicht ganz in der Taille sitzen haben, geht man vom Grundschnitt ca. 4 bis 6 cm nach unten. An dieser neuen Taillenlinie trägt man dann die gewünschte Breite – in diesem Fall 6 cm – für die gürtelförmige Passe ab.

3-4. Der Abnäher des Grundmodells muss im Papierschnitt zugelegt werden, der Abnäherinhalt also entfernt werden, um die Passe an die runde Taillenform anzupassen und gleichzeitig unschöne Abnähernähte zu vermeiden. Das Papier wird zu diesem Zweck an den Abnäherlinien geknickt und aufeinander gelegt, so rundet sich die Passe, und die Schnittkanten werden entsprechend ausgeglichen. Es ist wichtig darauf zu achten, dass an sämtlichen Ecken der Außenkante, sowohl an der Hinteren als auch der Vorderen Mitte und der Seitennaht, ein rechter Winkel beibehalten wird.

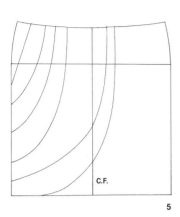

C.F.

5

6

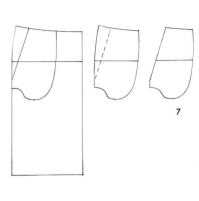

7

5-6. When the folds and the rounded border – the front edge of the hem – are marked up, you work, with this pattern as with the previous pattern, on the whole cut-out and not only on the half front part as with the basic skirt cut-out. The positions of the folds as well as their length and shape conform to the desired draft. This pattern has in every case three side folds and a slanting pocket opening.

7. The pocket pouch is drawn in as large as a palm starting from the side seam. The inner pouch goes up to the side seam and almost replaces the skirt part falling away because of the slanting opening. The outer pouch which can be cut from lining is added to the opening edge. Both pouch parts are closed together in the curve and caught in together with the side seam and band.

8. Now the fold lines are cut and opened up; the cut-out parts remain connected to the side seam, here the folds run in. For aesthetic reasons, you avoid any stitching with the yoke; therefore the front part of the yoke is carried to the back part and linked with the back part of the yoke, i.e. both cut-out parts are fixed together.

5-6. Lorsque les plis auront été marqués et le contour aura été arrondi –la partie avant de l'ourlet–, il faut alors travailler sur la coupe complète de même que sur le modèle précédent, et pas seulement sur le milieu avant comme c'était le cas sur le patron de base de la jupe. Les positions des plis, ainsi que leur forme et leur longueur, sont réalisés suivant le modèle désiré. Ce modèle présente trois plis latéraux et une poche oblique.

7. La poche sera marquée par des repères partant du côté et sa taille sera celle d'une grande assiette. La poche intérieure se prolongera jusqu'à la couture latérale et recouvrira pratiquement toute la pièce de la jupe éliminée par l'ouverture oblique. La poche extérieure, qui peut être découpée en tissu de doublure, commence au bord de l'ouverture. Les deux parties de la poche se refermeront au niveau de la ceinture corset et de la couture latérale, et seront reliées entre elles.

8. Les lignes des plis seront ensuite découpées et pliées. Les pièces de coupe sont reliées entre elles par la couture latérale, où commenceront les plis. Pour des raisons esthétiques, il faut éviter tout type de couture sur la ceinture corset. La ceinture

5-6. Wenn die Falten und der runde Abstich – die vordere Kante des Saums – markiert werden, arbeitet man bei diesem wie auch schon beim vorhergehenden Modell am ganzen Schnitt und nicht nur am halben Vorderteil wie beim Rockgrundschnitt. Die Positionen der Falten als auch deren Länge und Form richten sich nach dem gewünschten Entwurf. Dieses Modell besitzt jeweils drei seitliche Falten und einen schrägen Tascheneingriff.

7. Der Taschenbeutel wird handtellergroß von der Seitennaht ausgehend eingezeichnet. Der Innenbeutel geht dabei bis zur Seitennaht und ersetzt quasi das durch den schrägen Eingriff wegfallende Rockteil. Der Außenbeutel, der aus Futterstoff geschnitten werden kann, setzt an der Eingriffskante an. Beide Beutelteile werden zusammen in der Rundung geschlossen und in der Seitennaht und im Bund mitgefasst.

8. Nun werden die Faltenlinien eingeschnitten und aufgedreht; die Schnittteile bleiben an der Seitennaht zusammenhängend, hier werden die Falten einlaufen. Aus ästhetischen Gründen vermeidet man bei der Passe jegliche Nähte, deshalb wird die Vorderteilpasse am Rückenteil weitergeführt und

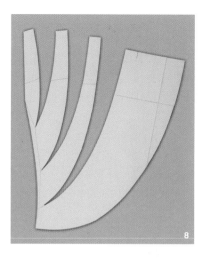

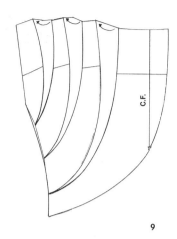

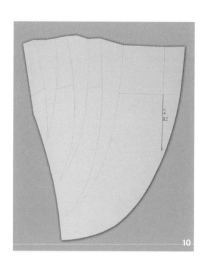

9-10. By cutting into the fold lines, freely swinging cut-out parts are created which only hang together on the side seam with the rest of the cut-out part. These are now positioned according to fold content, i.e. the amount decided by the desired depth of the fold. All cut-out parts are spliced with additional paper. The new front part of the pattern emerges. As the next step, the side seam is evened out, i.e. the corners are drawn in and cut. Then the paper is folded in the desired fold type and direction and the cut edges are balanced out, i.e. the waistline is cut straight in its folded condition. Jagged edges can thus emerge on the waistline when opening out which must be heeded at all costs when cutting out the fabric. The folds need exactly this content for the best layout when folded.

avant se prolonge donc jusque dans le dos et est reliée à la ceinture du dos, de sorte que les deux pièces de coupe restent collées.

9-10. En découpant les lignes de pli, des pièces de coupe se détachent et restent suspendues, avec les pièces de coupe restantes sur la couture latérale. Celles-ci se déplaceront grâce au volume des plis, c'est-à-dire, grâce à l'ensemble de la profondeur souhaitée au niveau des plis. Toutes les pièces de coupe seront collées avec du papier supplémentaire. Nous avons alors créé la nouvelle partie avant du modèle. Il faudra ensuite égaliser la couture latérale, c'est-à-dire, marquer et découper les angles. Le papier sera alors plié suivant le type de pli et le sens souhaités, et les bords de coupe seront égalisés de façon à ce que la ligne de la taille soit coupée droite avec le papier plié. Il se peut alors qu'au moment de déplier le papier, des dentelures apparaissent sur la ligne de la taille. Ces dentelures devront aussi absolument être prises en compte au moment de couper le tissu. Les plis ont précisément besoin de ce volume pour avoir une position optimale lorsqu'ils seront rabattus.

mit der Rückenteilpasse verbunden, also beide Schnittteile zusammengeklebt.

9-10. Durch das Einschneiden der Faltenlinien entstehen frei schwingende Schnittteile, die nur noch an der Seitennaht mit dem restlichen Schnittteil zusammenhängen. Diese werden nun mit dem Falteninhalt, also dem Betrag der sich aus der gewünschten Tiefe der Falte ergibt, verschoben. Sämtliche Schnittteile werden mit zusätzlichem Papier unterklebt. Das neue Modellvorderteil ist entstanden. Als Nächstes wird die Seitennaht ausgeglichen, d.h. die Ecken werden ausgezeichnet und beschnitten. Dann wird das Papier in der gewünschten Faltenart und Richtung geknickt und die Schnittkanten werden ausgeglichen, also die Taillenlinie in gefaltetem Zustand gerade abgeschnitten. Dadurch können an der Taillenlinie beim Aufklappen Zacken entstehen, die unbedingt auch beim Stoffzuschnitt beachtet werden müssen. Die Falten benötigen genau diesen Inhalt, um im gefalteten Zustand optimal zu liegen.

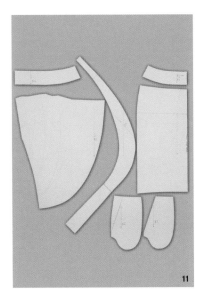

11. The finished cut-out parts: front and back part, front yoke, front and back part of the band yoke as well as inner and outer pocket pouch.

12. You should at all costs ensure that a right angle is always maintained on all corners of all cut-out parts, as only in this way can the fabric parts be linked with each other without pointed or flat angles emerging.

13. Curves in the fabric spread easily. You should therefore ensure when sewing a skirt that you put sufficient markers for the bias and attach the yoke at regular intervals.

11. Les pièces de coupe terminées : partie avant et dos, partie avant de ceinture corset, liaison entre cette dernière et le dos ainsi que poches intérieure et extérieure.

12. Il faut veiller à ce que tous les angles de toutes les pièces de coupe soient droits, puisque c'est la seule façon de pouvoir relier les pièces de tissu entre elles, sans que ne se forment des saillies ou des angles plats.

13. Les courbures du tissu s'agrandissent facilement. Il est pour cela important, au moment de coudre la jupe, d'avoir laissé suffisamment de lignes transversales et d'avoir relié les ceintures corset de manière régulière.

11. Die fertigen Schnittteile: Vorder- und Rückenteil, Frontpasse, Vorder- und Rückenteil-Bundpasse sowie Innen- und Außentaschenbeutel.

12. Man sollte unbedingt darauf achten, dass an sämtlichen Ecken aller Schnittteile immer ein rechter Winkel beibehalten wird, denn nur so können die Stoffteile miteinander verbunden werden, ohne dass spitze oder flache Winkel entstehen.

13. Rundungen im Stoff dehnen sich leicht aus. Daher sollte man beim Nähen des Rockes darauf achten, genügend Querzeichen zu setzen und die Passe regelmäßig anzustecken.

The basic pattern for dresses
Patron de base de robe
Der Kleidergrundschnitt

Example in size 12/14

BC Bust circumference 92 – 46 – 23 – 11.5 cm
WAC Waist circumference 72 – 36 – 18 cm
HC Hip circumference 100 – 50 cm

C Collar (*1/10 of the 1/2 BC + 2 cm*) 6.6 cm
BAH Back height 20.5 cm
BL Back length 41.8 cm
BL + HD Hip depth 62.6 cm
BD Bust depth 28.9 cm
FL Front length 45.9 cm

BAW Back width 17 cm
AD Armhole diameter (*1/8 BC % 1.5 cm*) 10 cm
BW Bust width (*1/4 BC % 4 cm*) 19 cm

The basic pattern for dresses is the basis for dresses and tops and is often also used as a starting point for jackets and coats. Since you are not creating a "second skin" but a covering around the body, you must not forget to add the following allowances to the measurements taken:

BAH Back height + *1 cm width allowance* = 21.5 cm
BAW Back width + *0.5 cm width allowance* = 17.5 cm
AD Armhole diameter + *1.5 cm width allowance* = 11.5 cm
BW Bust width + *1.5 cm width allowance* = 20.5 cm
1/2 BC Bust circumference (*BAW + AD + BW*) 46 cm + *3.5 cm width allowance* = 49.5 cm
SW Shoulder width 12.4 cm + *0.5 cm allowance of the back width* = 12.9 cm front shoulder width, + *0.6 cm easing width* = 13.5 cm rear shoulder width
ABC Angle of bust dart 16°

Exemple pour une taille 42

TP Tour de poitrine 92 – 46 – 23 – 11,5 cm
TT Tour de taille 72 – 36 – 18 cm
TH Tour de hanches 100 - 50 cm

C Col (*1/10 de 1/2 TP + 2 cm*) 6,6 cm
HD Hauteur du dos 20,5 cm
LD Longueur de dos 41,8 cm
LD + LTB Longueur taille-bassin 62,6 cm
PP Profondeur de poitrine 28,9 cm
LDe Longueur de devant 45,9 cm

CD Carrure dos 17 cm
DE Diamètre d'emmanchure (*1/8 TP % 1,5 cm*) 10 cm
LP Largeur de poitrine (*1/4 TP % 4 cm*) 19 cm

Le patron de base de robe est le support à partir duquel sont créés des robes et des hauts, et est également fréquemment utilisé comme patron de départ pour des vestes et des manteaux. Pour ne pas créer une « seconde peau » mais plutôt une enveloppe qui recouvre le corps, il ne faut pas oublier d'ajouter aux mesures prises, les valeurs suivantes :

HD Hauteur du dos + *1 cm de plus* = 21,5 cm
CD Carrure dos + *0,5 cm de plus* = 17,5 cm
DE Diamètre d'emmanchure + *1,5 cm de plus* = 11,5 cm
LP Largeur de poitrine + *1,5 cm de plus* = 20,5 cm
1/2 TP Tour de poitrine (*CD + DE + LP*) 46 cm + *3,5 cm de plus* = 49,5 cm
LE Longueur d'épaule 12,4 cm + *0,5 cm de plus que la carrure dos* = 12,9 cm largeur des épaules devant, + *0,6 cm de plus en largeur* = 13,5 cm largeur des épaules dans le dos
APP Angle de pince de poitrine 16°

Beispiel in Größe 40

BU Brustumfang 92 – 46 – 23 – 11,5 cm
TU Taillenumfang 72 – 36 – 18 cm
HU Hüftumfang 100 – 50 cm

HS Halsspiegel (*1/10 des 1/2 BU + 2 cm*) 6,6 cm
RH Rückenhöhe 20,5 cm
RL Rückenlänge 41,8 cm
RL + HT Hüfttiefe 62,6 cm
BT Brusttiefe 28,9 cm
VL Vorderlänge 45,9 cm

RB Rückenbreite 17 cm
AD Armlochdurchmesser (*1/8 BU % 1,5 cm*) 10 cm
BB Brustbreite (*1/4 BU % 4 cm*) 19 cm

Der Kleidergrundschnitt ist die Basis für Kleider und Oberteile und wird oft auch als Ausgangsgrundschnitt für Jacken und Mäntel verwendet. Da man keine „zweite Haut", sondern eine den Körper umgebende Hülle kreiert, darf man nicht vergessen, zu den gemessenen Maßen folgende Zugaben hinzuzufügen:

RH Rückenhöhe + *1 cm Weitenzugabe* = 21,5 cm
RB Rückenbreite + *0,5 cm Weitenzugabe* = 17,5 cm
AD Armlochdurchmesser + *1,5 cm Weitenzugabe* = 11,5 cm
BB Brustbreite + *1,5 cm Weitenzugabe* = 20,5 cm
1/2 BU Brustumfang (*RB + AD + BB*) 46 cm + *3,5 cm Weitenzugabe* = 49,5 cm
SCHB Schulterbreite 12,4 cm+ *0,5 cm Zugabe der Rückenbreite* = 12,9 cm vordere Schulterbreite,+ *0,6 cm Einhalteweite* = 13,5 cm hintere Schulterbreite
WBA Winkel Brustabnäher 16°

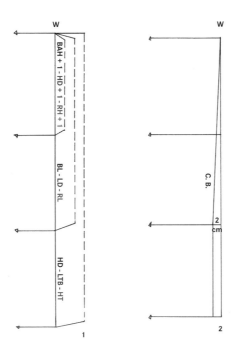

1. Pattern drawing begins by drawing a vertical line down from point W–the point corresponding with the first most prominent neckbone. Then, a line to the left at a right angle at exactly back height (incl. allowance), back length and hip depth measures is drawn. Thus, respectively, bustline, waistline and hipline are obtained.

2. Now the curve of the spine is registered by making a *2 cm adjustment* on the vertical line at the waistline and drawing a vertical line downwards over the hips to the hem.You link the point upwards with the tip of the spine. This line produces the seam in the centre back.

3. Starting from the point where the line of the centre back and the bust line meet, you can first of all measure the back width to the left and draw an angle upwards at this point. The measurement 2/3 of the armhole diameter is drawn away further along the bust line to the left and an angle line to the hem is drawn at this point. This line later serves for fixing the position of the side seam of the back part.
Now there follows a gap as large as you like, however not smaller than 6 cm so that later enough paper is available to separate

1. Commencer le patron en dessinant une ligne verticale sur laquelle sont déduites, du point de base du col (W) jusque vers le bas de la hauteur du dos (y compris la mesure supplémentaire), la longueur du dos et la longueur taille-bassin, et tracer sur chacune d'elles une ligne angulaire vers la gauche. Nous obtenons ainsi les lignes de poitrine, de taille et de hanches.

2. Relever ensuite la courbure de la colonne vertébrale en *ajustant de 2 cm* la ligne verticale au niveau de la ligne de la taille et en traçant une ligne verticale vers le bas sur les hanches jusqu'à l'ourlet. Ce point recoupe dans la partie supérieure le point de base du col. Cette ligne nous donne la couture arrière centrale.

3. À partir du point où se recoupent la ligne de milieu du dos et la ligne de poitrine, mesurer tout d'abord la carrure dos vers la gauche, puis tracer en ce point une ligne angulaire vers le haut. Également sur la ligne de poitrine, ôter vers la gauche 2/3 du diamètre d'emmanchure et en ce point, tracer une ligne angulaire jusqu'à l'ourlet. Cette ligne servira plus tard de point de repère pour la couture latérale de la pièce du dos.

1. Die Grundschnittzeichnung beginnt mit einer senkrechten Linie, auf der vom Wirbelpunkt (W) abwärts die Rückenhöhe (inkl. Zugabe), die Rückenlänge und die Hüfttiefe abgetragen und jeweils eine Winkellinie nach links gezogen werden. So entstehen Brustlinie, Taille und Hüftlinie.

2. Nun wird die Wirbelsäulenrundung erfasst, indem man an der senkrechten Linie auf der Taillenlinie *2 cm einstellt* und eine senkrechte Line über die Hüfte bis zum Saum nach unten zieht. Nach oben hin verbindet man den Punkt mit dem Wirbelpunkt. Diese Linie ergibt die Naht der Hinteren Mitte.

3. Vom Punkt ausgehend, in dem sich die Linie der Hinteren Mitte und die Brustlinie schneiden, misst man nun zuerst die Rückenbreite nach links ab und zieht an dieser Stelle eine Winkellinie nach oben. Weiter auf der Brustlinie nach links wird nun das Maß 2/3 des Armlochdurchmessers abgetragen und in diesem Punkt eine Winkellinie bis zum Saum gezogen. Diese Linie dient später der Orientierung für die Seitennaht des Rückenteils.
Nun folgt ein beliebig großer Zwischenraum, allerdings nicht kleiner als 6 cm, damit später genug Papier zur Verfügung

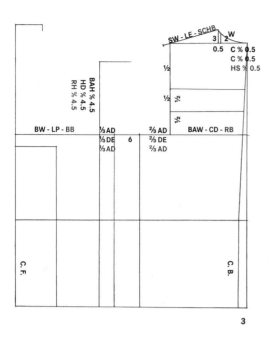

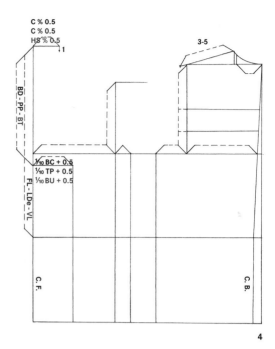

3

4

the front and back part from each other without problem.

Further along the bust line is the remaining third of the armhole diameter, the vertical line here is the so-called fore-arm line. Then the bust width is drawn out, and now the centre front is reached.

Here, you should briefly pause and carry out a test measurement for safety. The bust circumference without the gap must amount to 49.5 cm in this case.

When the framework is prepared from lines at an angle, you begin with the construction of the rear neckline by measuring the amount of the collar % 0.5 cm i.e. 6.1 cm to the left and 2 cm upwards and linking both points to a line.

A further 0.5 cm to the left, you then draw a parallel of 3 cm – here the rear neckline begins which is drawn round with the curve ruler.

At the starting point of the neckline, the rear shoulder line is also added, the length of which is now cut out over the point of the back rectangle. It is worth observing that the rear shoulder seam is 0.6 cm longer than the front one. This fullness is eased when sewing together and provides a better fit for the shoulder.

The horizontal halving of the back rectangle – the area between the back height

Laisser ensuite un espace intermédiaire, de la taille souhaitée mais d'au moins 6 cm , afin de disposer de suffisamment de papier pour séparer sans difficulté les pièces de devant et du dos.

Sur la ligne de poitrine se trouve également le tiers restant du diamètre d'emmanchure, cette ligne verticale s'appelle la ligne avant de la manche. La largeur de poitrine est alors retranchée pour se situer au centre de la partie avant.

Il convient ici de s'arrêter brièvement et par sécurité de réaliser une mesure d'essai. Le tour de poitrine sans espace intermédiaire doit mesurer dans ce cas 49,5 cm.

Une fois la structure de lignes angulaires complétée, il faut alors commencer à dessiner la partie arrière du col en mesurant à partir du point de base de celui-ci le total du col % 0,5 cm, c'est-à-dire 6,1 cm vers la gauche et 2 cm vers le haut, en obtenant ainsi une ligne entre ces deux points.

À 0,5 cm vers la gauche, une parallèle de 3 cm est tracée : ici commence la partie arrière du col, qui doit être tracé de manière arrondie à l'aide d'un patron à courbes.

La ligne arrière des épaules commence également au point de départ du col et sa longueur doit être ensuite retranchée en passant par le point du rectangle du dos.

steht, um Vorder- und Rückenteil problemlos voneinander zu trennen.

Weiter auf der Brustlinie liegt das restliche Drittel des Armlochdurchmessers, die senkrechte Linie hier ist die sogenannte Armvortrittslinie. Dann wird die Brustbreite abgetragen, und jetzt ist die Vordere Mitte erreicht.

Hier sollte man kurz einhalten und zur Sicherheit eine Testmessung durchführen. Der Brustumfang ohne Zwischenraum muss in diesem Falle 49,5 cm betragen.

Wenn das Gerüst aus Winkellinien fertig ist, beginnt man mit der Konstruktion des hinteren Halsloches, indem man vom Wirbelpunkt aus den Betrag des Halsspiegels % 0,5 cm, also 6,1 cm nach links und 2 cm nach oben, abmisst und beide Punkte zu einer Linie verbindet.

Weitere 0,5 cm nach links versetzt, zieht man dann eine Parallele von 3 cm – hier beginnt das Hintere Halsloch, das rund mit dem Kurvenlineal ausgezeichnet wird.

Am Anfangspunkt des Halsloches setzt auch die hintere Schulterlinie an, deren Länge nun über den Punkt des Rückenrechteckes abgetragen wird. Es gilt zu beachten, dass die hintere Schulternaht 0,6 cm länger ist als die vordere. Diese Mehrweite wird beim Zusammennähen eingehalten und sorgt für einen besseren Sitz der Schulter.

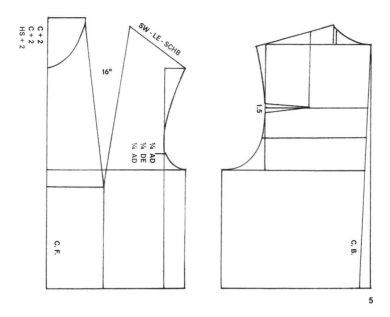

C + 2
C + 2
HS + 2

16°

SW - LE - SCHB

¼ AD
¼ DE
¼ AD

1.5

C. F.

C. B.

5

and the tip of the spine – gives the later dart position; the rear sleeve insertion point is at the quarter distance.

The front shoulder emerges by measuring the amount of the back height % 4.5 cm here 17 cm, upwards on the fore-arm line vertically, and at this point cutting a guiding line of approx. 10 cm to the right.

4. At the centre front you measure the amount of the front length upwards from the waist out, bend to the right for the amount of collar % 0.5 cm to go 1 cm downwards again there. Here, the left edge of the bust dart begins.

At the centre front, you also measure the bust depth from above downwards and bend 1/10 of the bust circumference + 0.5 cm to the right.

5. The front neckline is made by measuring the collar + 2 cm from the highest point of the centre front line downwards and then rounding off the pattern.

The left edge of the bust dart is drawn to the bust apex, subtracting the corresponding angle depending on the size of garment, in this case it is 16º, the same is done to the right edge of the same length.

Then you make the front shoulder width of 12.9 cm meet the angle line and mark the

Il faut tenir compte du fait que la couture de l'épaule à l'arrière est 0,6 cm plus longue que celle à l'avant. Cette différence de largeur se maintient au moment de les coller et permet une certaine flexibilité au niveau des épaules.

À partir de la division horizontale en deux du rectangle du dos -la surface comprise entre le haut du dos et le point de base du col- nous obtenons la position où devront au maximum être placées les pinces, à un quart se trouve le point arrière d'insertion de la manche.

La partie avant de l'épaule s'obtient en mesurant verticalement au niveau de la ligne avant de la manche la hauteur du dos % 4,5 cm, ici 17 cm, et à partir de ce point, une ligne auxiliaire d'environ 10 cm est dressée vers la droite.

4. Au centre du milieu avant, effectuer la mesure vers le haut à partir de la taille, de la longueur de taille devant, puis tracer de manière inclinée vers la droite la grandeur du col % 0,5 cm, puis de nouveau vers le bas de 1 cm. Le côté gauche de la pince de la poitrine commencera à partir de ce point.

Également au centre du milieu avant, mesurer de haut en bas la hauteur de poitrine et tracer de manière inclinée

Die waagrechte Halbierung des Rückenrechtecks – dem Bereich zwischen der Rückenhöhe und dem Wirbelpunkt – ergibt die spätere Abnäherlage; bei einem Viertel befindet sich der hintere Ärmeleinsatzpunkt.

Die vordere Schulter entsteht, indem man an der Armvortrittslinie senkrecht den Betrag der Rückenhöhe % 4,5 cm, hier 17 cm, nach oben abmisst und an diesem Punkt eine Hilfslinie von ca. 10 cm nach rechts abträgt.

4. An der Vorderen Mitte misst man von der Taille aus den Betrag der Vorderlänge nach oben, winkelt nach rechts den Betrag des Halsspiegels % 0,5 cm ab, um von dort wieder 1cm nach unten zu gehen. Hier wird der linke Schenkel des Brustabnähers beginnen.

Ebenfalls an der Vorderen Mitte misst man von oben nach unten die Brusttiefe ab und winkelt 1/10 des Brustumfangs + 0,5 cm nach rechts.

5. Das vordere Halsloch entsteht, indem man den Halsspiegel + 2 cm von der höchsten Stelle der vorderen Mitte-Linie nach unten misst und dann den Ausschnitt ausrundet.

Der linke Schenkel des Brustabnähers wird zum Brustpunkt gezogen, je nach

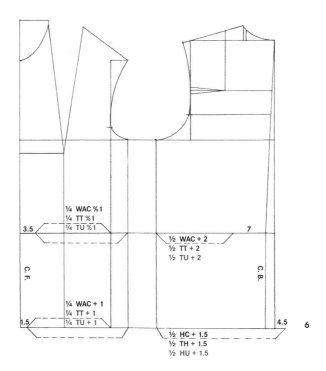

armhole. Taking the measurement 1/4 of the armhole diameter on the fore-arm line from the bust line upwards results in the front sleeve inset marker.

In the case of the rear arm cut-out, the 1.5 cm deep dart is now drawn in on the halved back rectangle and the cut-out drawn round. You must ensure that both shoulder lines pass into the armhole curve at a right angle, otherwise you will form unattractive points when sewing the parts together.

The throat and shoulder area is thus complete – the whole basic pattern is drawn up according to the bust circumference measurement.

6. Allowing for the obviously differing circumferences of the body, you add darts to the waist to reduce its width and add volume to the curvature of the hip.

The darts are drawn in by going out at the waistline of the front part, beginning at the fore-arm line, to the left *1/4 of the waist circumference % 1 cm* and measuring the remaining amount up to the centre front. The corresponding difference, here 3.5 cm, is then removed as darts.

The volume for the dart at the hipline is ascertained by adding *2 cm to the result from the waist formula* (*1/4 of the waist circumference % 1 cm*), and in this way

1/10 du tour de poitrine + 0,5 cm vers la droite.

5. La partie avant du col est obtenue en mesurant vers le bas du col + 2 cm à partir du point le plus haut de la ligne centrale avant et en arrondissant ensuite l'encolure.

Le côté gauche de la pince de la poitrine est tracé jusqu'au point le plus saillant de cette dernière, en retranchant l'angle correspondant selon la taille du vêtement, dans ce cas 16º, et est complété avec la même longueur du côté droit.

La longueur des épaules avant de 12,9 cm est alors reliée à la ligne angulaire et le poignet est marqué avec des repères. Si la grandeur 1/4 du diamètre d'emmanchureest mesurée vers le haut au niveau de la ligne avant de la manche et à partir de la ligne de la poitrine, nous obtenons le repère avant d'insertion de la manche.

La pince de 1,5 cm de profondeur est ensuite marquée sur l'emmanchure arrière dans le rectangle du dos divisé en deux et l'emmanchure est arrondie. Il faudra veiller à ce que les deux lignes des épaules arrivent en angle droit sur la courbure du poignet, sinon des pointes inesthétiques risquent de se former en collant les pièces.

Ainsi se termine la zone du col et des épaules. L'ensemble du patron de base

Konfektionsgröße der entsprechende Winkel, hier 16°, abgetragen und um den rechten Schenkel in gleicher Länge ergänzt.

Dann lässt man die vordere Schulterbreite von 12,9 cm auf die Winkellinie treffen und zeichnet das Armloch aus. Das Maß 1/4 des Armlochdurchmessers auf der Armvortrittslinie von der Brustlinie aus nach oben gemessen ergibt dabei das vordere Ärmeleinsatzzeichen.

Beim hinteren Armausschnitt wird nun der 1,5 cm tiefe Abnäher auf dem halbierten Rückenrechteck eingezeichnet und der Ausschnitt rund ausgezeichnet. Es ist darauf zu achten, dass beide Schulterlinien mit einem rechten Winkel in die Armlochrundung übergehen, sonst bilden sie beim Zusammennähen der Teile unschöne Spitzen.

Der Hals- bis Schulterbereich ist somit fertig gestellt – der gesamte Grundschnitt ist nach dem Brustumfangsmaß aufgestellt.

6. Den offensichtlich abweichenden Umfängen des Körpers Rechnung tragend, fügt man an der Taille zur Weitenreduzierung Abnäher ein und gibt an der Hüftrundung Volumen zu.

Die Abnäher werden eingezeichnet, indem man an der Taillenlinie des Vorderteils, beginnend an der Armvortrittslinie, nach links *1/4 des Taillenumfangs % 1 cm*

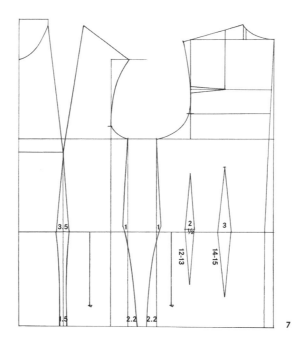

7

you obtain 19 cm. The remaining amount for the centre front thus works out at 1.5 cm.

Now the darts for the back part are drawn in; for this you go out from the left outer line to the right *1/2 of the waist circumference + 2 cm* and count the rest of the amount to the centre back, here 7 cm. At the hipline you go out to the right *1/2 of the hip circumference + 1.5 cm*. In this way, you get beyond the basic pattern and establish therefore an excess amount of 4.5 cm which has to be added to the hipline.

7. Here you see the distribution of the slack and the position of the darts. On the line under the bust apex, there lies the dart for the front part with a depth of 3.5 cm in the waist and 1.5 cm on the hips; the darts are drawn in slightly curved from the waistline to do justice to the increasingly convex shape of the body.

The slack of the back part, 7 cm at the waist and 4.5 cm at the hips, is distributed between both side seams and two darts. In this way, you conform best to the shape of the body and also achieve not having the darts at the back amounting to over 3 cm which would not stand in good stead for the correct fit of the pattern.

In the case of the dart close to the side seam, it's at the deepest point of the body

est tracé en fonction de la dimension du tour de poitrine.

6. Étant donné les variations des courbes du corps qui existent, des pinces sont mises en place au niveau de la taille pour réduire la largeur et du volume est ajouté dans la courbure des hanches.

Les pinces sont marquées en retranchant vers la gauche sur la ligne de la taille de la pièce de devant, à partir de la ligne avant de la manche, *1/4 du tour de taille % 1 cm* et en mesurant le reste de la grandeur vers le milieu avant. L'écart correspondant, dans ce cas 3,5 cm, est alors enlevé sous forme de pinces.

Le volume des pinces de la ligne des hanches est calculé en ajoutant *2 cm au résultat de la formule de la taille (1/4 du tour de taille % 1 cm)*, pour finalement obtenir 19 cm. La grandeur restante au milieu avant est donc de 1,5 cm.

Les pinces de la pièce du dos sont ensuite marquées en partant pour cela de la ligne extérieure gauche *1/2 du tour de taille + 2 cm* vers la droite et en mesurant le reste vers le centre de la partie arrière, dans ce cas 7 cm. *1/2 du tour de hanches + 1,5 cm* est compté vers la droite sur la ligne des hanches. Le patron de base est ainsi terminé et un supplément de 4,5 cm doit être ajouté à la ligne des hanches.

abträgt und den verbleibenden Betrag bis zur vorderen Mitte misst. Die entsprechende Differenz, hier 3,5 cm, wird dann als Abnäher weggenommen.

Das Volumen für den Abnäher an der Hüftlinie wird durch Hinzugeben von *2 cm zum Ergebnis der Taillenformel (1/4 des Taillenumfangs % 1 cm)* ermittelt, und so erhält man 19 cm. Der Restbetrag zur Vorderen Mitte beträgt somit 1,5 cm.

Nun werden die Abnäher für das Rückenteil eingezeichnet; dafür trägt man von der linken äußeren Linie nach rechts *1/2 des Taillenumfangs + 2 cm* ab und misst den Restbetrag zur Hinteren Mitte, hier 7 cm. An der Hüftlinie trägt man nach rechts *1/2 des Hüftumfangs + 1,5 cm* ab. Auf diese Weise gelangt man über den Grundschnitt hinaus, stellt also einen Überbetrag von 4,5 cm fest, der an der Hüftlinie hinzu gegeben werden muss.

7. Hier sieht man nun die Ausfallverteilung und die Lage der Abnäher. Auf der Linie unter der Brustspitze liegt der Vorderteilabnäher mit einer Tiefe von 3,5 cm in der Taille und 1,5 cm an der Hüfte; ab der Taillenlinie wird der Abnäher leicht gerundet ausgezeichnet, um der zunehmend konvex werdenden Körperform gerecht zu werden.

Der Ausfall des Rückenteils, 7 cm an der Taille und 4,5 cm an der Hüfte, wird auf

and like with the procedure for the basic pattern for the skirt the widest part of the dart is therefore positioned 1/2 cm over the waistline.

8. It is recommended that you move the rear armhole dart into the shoulder and the front bust dart into the side seam, since there the seams are less bothersome both visually and also for further work at the cutting out (e.g. collars).
The bust and waist darts in the front part should in any case be shortened by *approx. 2 cm* before the cutting out so that they do not end directly at the bust apex.

9. This drawing shows the parts ready for cutting out the dresses. With all seam and dart alterations you are to ensure that the further you deviate from the original position, the higher the risk of spoiling the shape of the yoke.

7. Nous pouvons observer ici la distribution du surplus et la position des pinces. La pince de la pièce de devant se trouve sur la ligne qui passe en dessous du point le plus saillant de la poitrine, avec une profondeur de 3,5 cm au niveau de la taille et 1,5 cm au niveau des hanches. Les pinces sont tracées à partir de la ligne de la taille de manière arrondie afin qu'elles correspondent à la convexité croissante de la forme du corps.
Le surplus de la pièce du dos, 7 cm au niveau de la taille et 4,5 cm au niveau des hanches, se distribue entre les deux coutures latérales et deux pinces. Ainsi, le patron s'ajuste parfaitement à la forme du corps et les pinces arrière présentent une profondeur inférieure à 3 cm, car au-delà elles empêchent un bon ajustement au corps.
Au niveau des pinces proches de la couture latérale se trouve le point le plus profond du corps et, de même que pour le patron de base de la jupe, le point le plus profond de la pince 1/2 cm se situe au-dessus de la ligne de la taille.

8. Il est recommandé de déplacer la pince arrière du poignet sur l'épaule et la pince avant de la poitrine sur la couture latérale, car de cette manière, les coutures sont moins gênantes tant d'un point de vue visuel que pour le reste de la coupe (par ex. le col).
Les pinces de la poitrine et de la taille de la pièce de devant doivent toujours être raccourcies avant la coupe *d'environ 2 cm*, pour qu'elles ne se terminent pas sur le point de la poitrine.

9. Ce dessin montre les pièces du patron de la robe prêtes pour la coupe. À chaque fois que les coutures et les pinces seront déplacées, il faudra tenir compte du fait que plus elles s'éloignent de la position d'origine, plus le risque d'empirer la situation est important.

beide Seitennähte und zwei Abnäher verteilt. So entspricht man der Körperform am besten und erreicht zudem, dass die hinteren Abnäher nicht über 3 cm Tiefe betragen, was der Passform des Modells nicht zugute käme.
Beim Abnäher nahe der Seitennaht befindet sich die tiefste Stelle des Körpers und ähnlich wie beim Rockgrundschnitt wird daher die breiteste Abnähertiefe 1/2 cm über die Taillenlinie gesetzt.

8. Empfehlenswert ist es, den hinteren Armlochabnäher in die Schulter zu verlegen und den vorderen Brustabnäher in die Seitennaht, da dort die Nähte sowohl optisch als auch für die weitere Bearbeitung des Schnittes (z. B. Krägen) weniger stören.
Der Brust- und der Taillenabnäher im Vorderteil sollten in jedem Fall vor dem Zuschnitt um *ca. 2 cm* verkürzt werden, sodass sie nicht direkt auf dem Brustpunkt enden.

9. Diese Zeichnung zeigt die schnittfertigen Teile des Kleiderschnitts. Bei sämtlichen Naht- und Abnäherverlegungen ist zu beachten, dass je weiter man von der ursprünglichen Position abweicht, desto höher wird das Risiko einer Passformverschlechterung.

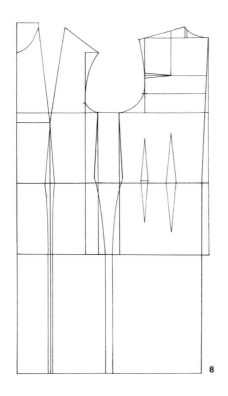

8

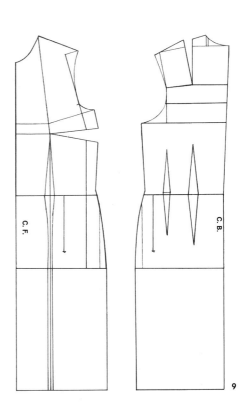

C. F.

C. B.

9

The basic pattern for the sleeve
Patron de base de manche
Der Ärmelgrundschnitt

SL Sleeve length 60 cm
SHH Sleeve head height (*BAH Back height %*
5.5 cm) 15.5 cm
SLW Sleeve width (*AD Armhole diameter +*
allowance 5 cm) 16.5 cm
SHW Sleeve hem width 23 cm

BAH Back height + *1 cm length allowance* =
21.5 cm
AD Armhole diameter + *1.5 cm width allowance*
= 11.5 cm

The basic pattern for the sleeve is a classic
head sleeve with one seam. It serves as
the basis for almost all sleeve types (two
seam sleeve, raglan sleeve, bat sleeve
etc.), even when it can often hardly be
recognized at the end. Since it represents
an item that needs to be flexible, i.e. the
arm should be well clothed both in movement and also in the suspended resting
position, its correct assembly and shaping
is not so easy and needs some practice.

10. Initially you draw a vertical line of 60
cm downwards. This line defines the starting point A and the end point D and represents the sleeve length. Starting from
Point A, you then cut along the height of
the sleeve head and obtain Point B.
If you now *halve* the length B – D and *re-*
duce this amount by 2 cm, then this results
in the reference for the elbow line C.
Starting from A again, you go along the
sleeve width to the right and obtain in this
way Point E. On the half of the length A –
E + *1 cm* there is the highest point of the
sleeve (Point F), which meets the shoulder
seam of the torso part when inserting the
sleeve.
Then you measure vertically from Point B
upwards *1/4 of the armhole diameter* and
in this way ascertain the inset marker for
the front part of the sleeve (Point G). You
obtain a further secondary construction
point (H) by going down vertically by the
amount of *1/4 of the armhole diameter +*
0.5 cm starting from Point E.

11. The left sleeve seam is drawn in by going along horizontally from Point B *1/3 of*
the armhole diameter to the left. From this
new point you measure the double sleeve
width, to the right and in this way obtain
the right sleeve seam.

LoM Longueur de manche 60 cm
HTM Hauteur de tête de manche (*HD Hauteur*
du dos % 5,5 cm) 15,5 cm
LaM Largeur de manche (*DE Diamètre*
d'emmanchure + plus 5 cm) 16,5 cm
LBM Largeur de bord de manche 23 cm

HD Hauteur du dos + *1 cm de plus* = 21,5 cm
DE Diametre d'emmanchure + *1,5 cm de plus*
= 11,5 cm

Le patron de base de manche correspond
à une manche droite classique à une couture. Il sert de support pour réaliser presque tout type de manche (manche à deux
coutures, manche raglan, manche chauve
souris, etc.), bien que cela ne se remarque à peine dans le résultat final. Puisqu'il
s'agit d'un élément mobile, c'est-à-dire
qu'il doit bien recouvrir le bras aussi bien
en mouvement que détaché au repos, sa
fabrication et sa correcte finition ne sont
pas si faciles et demandent une certaine
expérience.

10. Tracer tout d'abord une ligne verticale
vers le bas de 60 cm. Cette ligne définit le
point de départ A et le point final D, et représente la longueur de manche. À partir
du point A, retrancher la hauteur de tête
de manche pour obtenir le point B.
Diviser ensuite *par deux* le segment B –
D et *réduire cette grandeur de 2 cm*, pour
obtenir ainsi la référence pour la ligne du
coude C.
En partant de nouveau du point A, retrancher vers la droite la largeur de manche
pour obtenir le point E. Au milieu du segment A – E + *1 cm* se trouve le point le plus
haut de la manche (point F) qui, en mettant
les manches, se trouve au niveau de la couture de l'épaule de la pièce du tronc.
Mesurer alors à partir du point B verticalement vers le haut *1/4 du diametre d'em-*
manchure et calculer le repère avant d'insertion de la manche (point G). Un autre
point auxiliaire du dessin (H) est obtenu
en retranchant la grandeur *1/4 diametre*
d'emmanchure + 0,5 cm verticalement
vers le bas en partant d'en dessous du
point E.

11. La couture gauche de la manche doit
être marquée en retranchant *1/3 diame-*
tre d'emmanchure vers la gauche horizon-
talement à partir du point B. À partir de

ÄLG Ärmellänge 60 cm
ÄKH Ärmelkugelhöhe (*RH Rückenhöhe % 5,5 cm*)
15,5 cm
ÄB Ärmelbreite (*AD Armlochdurchmesser +*
Zugabe 5 cm) 16,5 cm
ÄSW Ärmelsaumweite 23 cm

RH Rückenhöhe + *1 cm Längenzugabe* = 21,5 cm
AD Armlochdurchmesser + *1,5 cm*
Weitenzugabe = 11,5 cm

Der Ärmelgrundschnitt ist ein klassischer
Kugelärmel mit einer Naht. Er dient als
Grundlage fast aller Ärmeltypen (Zweinahtärmel, Raglanärmel, Fledermaus etc.),
auch wenn er am Ende oft kaum noch zu
erkennen ist. Da er ein bewegliches Modul
darstellt, d.h. den Arm sowohl in Bewegung
als auch in hängender Ruhelage gut beklei-
den soll, ist seine korrekte Aufstellung und
Verarbeitung nicht so einfach und bedarf
einiger Übung.

10. Zunächst zieht man eine senkrechte
Linie von 60 cm nach unten. Diese Linie
definiert den Ausgangspunkt A und den
Endpunkt D und repräsentiert die Ärmel-
länge. Vom Punkt A ausgehend, trägt man
dann die Ärmelkugelhöhe ab und erhält
Punkt B.
Halbiert man nun die Strecke B – D und
reduziert diesen Betrag um 2 cm, so ergibt
sich die Referenz für die Ellenbogenlinie C.
Erneut von A ausgehend, trägt man nach
rechts die Ärmelbreite ab und erhält so
Punkt E. Auf der Hälfte der Strecke A – E +
1 cm befindet sich der höchste Punkt des
Ärmels (Punkt F), der beim Einsetzen der
Ärmel auf die Schulternaht des Rumpfteils
trifft.
Dann misst man vom Punkt B senkrecht
nach oben *1/4 des Armlochdurchmessers*
ab und ermittelt so das vordere Ärmeleinsatzzeichen (Punkt G). Einen weiteren
Hilfskonstruktionspunkt (H) erhält man
durch Abtragen des Betrages *1/4 des*
Armlochdurchmessers + 0,5 cm senkrecht
nach unten vom Punkt E ausgehend.

11. Die linke Ärmelnaht wird eingezeichnet,
indem man waagerecht von Punkt B *1/3*
des Armlochdurchmessers nach links abträgt. Von diesem neuen Punkt aus misst
man die doppelte Ärmelbreite, den Är-

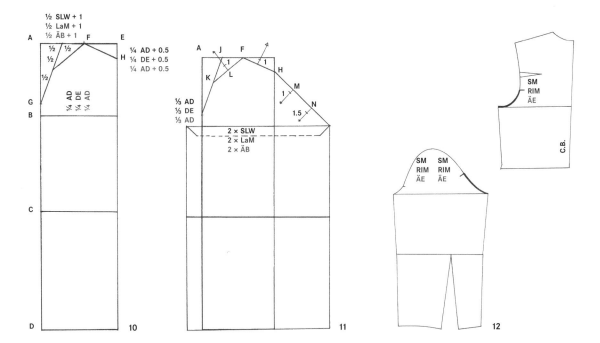

Now the curves of the curve-shaped head of the sleeve must be marked correctly, so you define three guiding points.

From the upper sleeve inset marker (Point F) you draw a line to the guiding point H, halve it and then establish a point *1 cm* over the line.

You ascertain Point J by halving length A - F. Then Point J is linked with the front inset marker (G) and this length halved again. Point K formed in this way is linked following this with the sleeve insertion point (F) and raised by *1 cm* at the half-way point (L).

Beginning at Point H, a line goes to the right side seam, where, divided into three, the starting points M and N are obtained for the two last guiding points. At the respective angle lines *1 cm* (M) *or 1.5 cm* (N) are now drawn away at a right angle and then the curves of the sleeve head are drawn in with the curve ruler.

12. The exact position of the rear sleeve inset marker is ascertained by measuring the rear armhole at the torso part from the side seam to the sleeve insert marker; then 1 cm is added to it and the placing incorporated on the sleeve pattern.

Now you should measure again with the tape measure the length of the sleeve head from the front to the rear sleeve inset marker and compare with the corresponding

ce nouveau point, mesurer la largeur de la manche double, le tour de la manche, vers la droite pour obtenir ainsi la couture droite de la manche.

Marquer ensuite correctement les contours courbés de la tête de la manche, en définissant pour cela trois points auxiliaires.

À partir du repère supérieur d'insertion de la manche (point F), tracer une ligne au niveau du point auxiliaire H, diviser en deux, puis déterminer un point *1 cm* sur la ligne.

Le point J est obtenu en divisant par deux le segment A - F, puis est relié au repère supérieur avant d'insertion de la manche (G), et ce segment est à nouveau divisé en deux. Le point K obtenu est ensuite relié au point d'insertion de la manche (F), et *1 cm* est ajouté au milieu (L) de ce segment.

À partir du point H, tracer une ligne allant à la couture latérale droite, la diviser en trois pour obtenir les points de départ M et N pour les deux derniers points auxiliaires. Sur les lignes angulaires correspondantes, retrancher alors *1 cm* (M) *ou 1,5 cm* (N) en angle droit, puis marquer les courbures de la tête de la manche avec un patron à courbes.

12. La position exacte du repère arrière d'insertion de la manche est calculée en

melumfang, nach rechts und erhält so die rechte Ärmelnaht.

Nun müssen die kurvenförmigen Ärmelkugelrundungen korrekt markiert werden, daher definiert man drei Hilfspunkte.

Vom oberen Ärmeleinsatzeichen (Punkt F) zieht man eine Linie zum Hilfspunkt H, halbiert sie und legt anschließend einen Punkt *1 cm* über der Linie fest.

Den Punkt J ermittelt man durch die Halbierung der Strecke A – F. Dann wird Punkt J mit dem vorderen Einsatzeichen (G) verbunden und diese Strecke erneut halbiert. Der so entstandene Punkt K wird im Folgenden mit dem Ärmeleinsatzpunkt (F) verbunden und auf halber Strecke (L) um *1 cm* erhöht.

Beginnend im Punkt H, führt eine Linie zur rechten Seitennaht, gedrittelt ergeben sich die Ausgangspunkte M und N für die beiden letzten Hilfspunkte. Auf den jeweiligen Winkellinien werden nun *1 cm* (M) *bzw. 1,5 cm* (N) im rechten Winkel abgetragen und anschließend die Ärmelkugelrundungen mit dem Kurvenlineal eingezeichnet.

12. Die genaue Position des hinteren Ärmeleinsatzeichens wird ermittelt, indem am Rumpfteil das hintere Armloch von der Seitennaht bis hin zum Ärmeleinsatzeichen ausgemessen wird; dann wird noch 1 cm hinzuaddiert und die Platzierung auf dem Ärmelschnitt eingetragen.

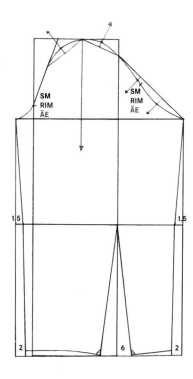

SM
RIM
ÄE

SM
RIM
ÄE

1.5   1.5

2   6   2   **13**

areas in the front and back torso part. A certain fullness of the sleeve of approx *10 percent* is envisaged and should be eased when sewing in, since the sleeve can fall better in this way.

13. The side seams are adjusted *1.5 cm* at the elbow line and *2 cm* at the hem respectively to lend the sleeve an attractive shape following the arm and achieve the desired sleeve hem width.
Then the hem width is measured again, the difference to the desired hem measurement gives the depth of the dart. This is drawn out on Line E from the elbow line and evenly distributed to the right and left.
Now you bend from the right dart edge to the side seam to obtain a rectangular hem again. Here the side seam shortens by a few millimeters. Remove this amount on the left side seam too and angle to the dart.

14. The complete single-seamed sleeve with darts in the hem.

mesurant le poignet arrière sur la pièce du tronc, à partir de la couture latérale jusqu'au repère d'insertion de la manche, ajouter ensuite 1 cm puis relever la mise en place de l'emmanchure.
À l'aide du mètre à ruban, mesurer la longueur de la tête de manche à partir du repère avant d'insertion de la manche jusqu'au repère arrière, et comparer avec la surface correspondante des pièces de devant et du dos. Une différence de largeur de la manche d'environ *10 pour cent* est intentionnelle et doit être maintenue, puisque la manche présente ainsi une retombée plus souple.

13. Les coutures latérales de la ligne du coude sont élaborées avec *1,5 cm* chacune, et *2 cm* au niveau du poignet, afin de donner une jolie forme à la manche qui s'adapte au contour du bras, et définir la largeur de poignet souhaitée.
Mesurer alors la largeur de fond, l'écart par rapport à la largeur de poignet souhaitée nous donne la profondeur de la pince. Celle-ci se retranche sur la ligne E à partir

Nun sollte man mit dem Maßband die Länge der Kugel vom vorderen zum hinteren Ärmeleinsatzzeichen nachmessen und mit den entsprechenden Bereichen im Vorder- und Rückrumpfteil vergleichen. Eine gewisse Mehrweite des Ärmels von ca. *10 Prozent* ist beabsichtigt und sollte beim Einnähen eingehalten werden, da der Ärmel so besser fallen kann.

13. Die Seitennähte an der Ellenbogenlinie werden jeweils *1,5 cm* und am Saum jeweils *2 cm* eingestellt, um dem Ärmel eine schöne, dem Arm folgende Form zu verleihen und die gewünschte Ärmelsaumweite zu erreichen.
Dann wird die Saumweite ausgemessen, die Differenz zum Wunschsaummaß ergibt die Abnähertiefe. Dieser wird auf der Linie E von der Ellenbogenlinie aus abgetragen und gleichmäßig nach rechts und links verteilt.
Jetzt winkelt man vom rechten Abnäherschenkel hin zur Seitennaht ab, um wieder einen rechtwinkligen Saum zu erhalten. Hier kürzt sich die Seitennaht um einige

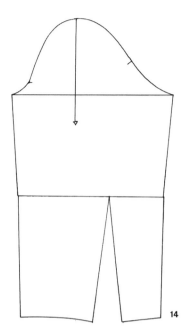

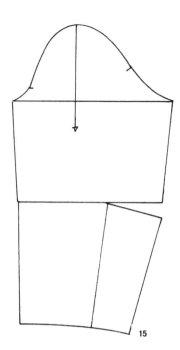

14

15

15. The dart can also be laid on the elbow line into the rear side seam and sewn there. The advantage of this variant is that the dart is shorter and therefore is not as obvious.

de la ligne du coude et se distribue uniformément à droite et à gauche.
Continuer ensuite de manière oblique du côté droit de la pince à la couture latérale afin d'obtenir à nouveau un poignet à angle droit. Raccourcir ici de quelques millimètres la couture latérale. Cette grandeur est également retranchée sur la couture latérale gauche, puis inclinée du côté de la pince.

14. Manche à une couture déjà préparée avec une pince au niveau du poignet.

15. La pince peut également être placée et cousue sur la ligne du coude de la couture latérale arrière. Cette opération a pour avantage de considérablement raccourcir la pince, qui se remarque donc moins.

Millimeter. Diesen Betrag auch auf der linken Seitennaht abtragen und zum Abnäherschenkel winkeln.

14. Der fertige Einnahtärmel mit Abnäher im Saum.

15. Der Abnäher kann auch auf der Ellenbogenlinie in die hintere Seitennaht gelegt und dort genäht werden. Der Vorteil dieser Variante ist es, dass der Abnäher wesentlich kürzer ist und dadurch weniger auffällt.

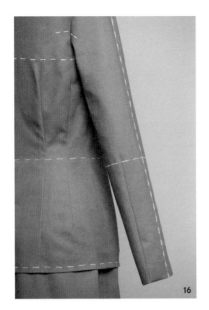

16

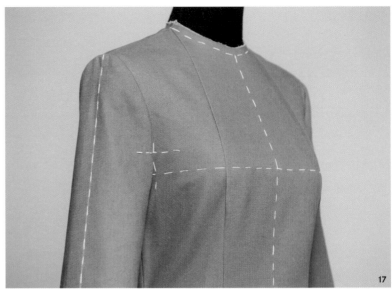

17

18

19

16-17. When inserting the sleeves, the insert markers should meet up with each other. However, it is often the case when trying on that a sleeve has to be somewhat shifted forwards or backwards to do justice to the respective posture. The shoulder width can also be corrected at the same time.

18-19. The darts in the back and front part provide an optimal fit to the body. Shoulder blades, curvature of the spine, waist and bust must often be individually adjusted.

16-17. En mettant en place la manche, les repères d'insertion doivent coïncider. Il arrive souvent que lors des essayages, il soit nécessaire de rallonger ou de raccourcir une manche afin que le vêtement s'ajuste correctement à la posture du corps. Il est également possible de corriger la longueur des épaules.

18-19. Les pinces des pièces de devant et de l'épaule permettent de parfaitement ajuster le vêtement au corps. Il est souvent nécessaire d'adapter individuellement les épaules, la courbure du dos, la taille et la poitrine.

16-17. Beim Einsetzen des Ärmels sollten die Einsatzzeichen aufeinander treffen. Nicht selten tritt aber bei der Anprobe der Fall auf, dass ein Ärmel etwas nach vorne oder hinten verschoben werden muss, um der jeweiligen Körperhaltung gerecht zu werden. Die Schulterbreite kann hierbei ebenfalls korrigiert werden.

18-19. Die Abnäher im Rücken- und Vorderteil sorgen für ein optimales Anliegen an den Körper. Schulterblätter, Wirbelsäulenkrümmung, Taille und Brust müssen oft noch individuell angepasst werden.

Shoulder-less dress with flared skirt
Robe sans manches avec jupe volantée
Schulterfreies Kleid mit Glockenrock

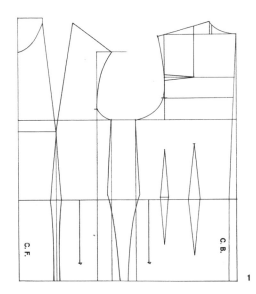

C. F.

C. B.

1

1. This dress prepared from the basic pattern consists of a gathered, symmetrical upper part and a flared skirt. A band links the front and back part and forms at the same time the length-adjustable straps. For this pattern an easily falling fabric would be advisable.

1. Cette robe créée à partir du patron de base présente une partie supérieure symétrique froncée et une jupe volantée. Un ruban relie les parties avant et arrière, et constitue également un cordon de longueur réglable. Ce modèle nécessite un tissu tombé.

1. Dieses aus dem Grundschnitt entwickelte Kleid besteht aus einem gerafften, symmetrischen Oberteil und einem Glockenrock. Ein Band verbindet Vorder- und Rückenteil und bildet zugleich die längenverstellbaren Träger. Für dieses Modell bietet sich ein leicht fallender Stoff an.

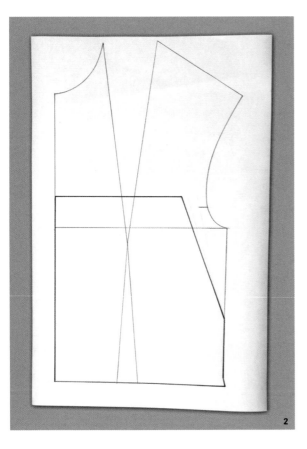

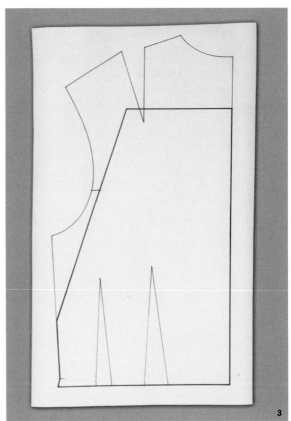

2. The basic pattern of the dress however can only be used for cutting out the upper part to the waistline. The height of the cut-out part as well as the depth of the arm-holes can be determined quite freely, how-ever you should not go below a minimum height in the case of the front part. It is help-ful to work it out from the bust and shoulder line as well as try out the measurements on the body itself.

3. As has already been done with the front, with the back part too you go by the basic pattern of the dress. The shape and height of the back part can differ here from the front part, however the length of the side seam where the front and back parts are sewn together, should correspond.

2. Pour la coupe de la partie supérieure, le patron de base de la robe ne peut être utilisé que jusqu'à la ligne de la taille. La hauteur de la coupe ainsi que la profon-deur jusqu'au bras peuvent facilement être déterminées, bien que dans la partie avant, une hauteur minimale obligatoire soit exigée. Il s'avère utile de se guider par rapport à la ligne de la poitrine et les épaules, ainsi que d'essayer les mesures directement sur le corps.

3. De même que sur la partie avant, le patron de base de la robe permet de se repérer sur la partie arrière. La forme et la hauteur de la partie arrière peuvent être différentes de la partie avant, mais la longueur des coutures latérales, qui relient les deux parties, doit coïncider pour les deux.

2. Der Grundschnitt des Kleides lässt sich für den Schnitt des Oberteils allerdings nur bis zur Taillenlinie verwenden. Die Höhe des Ausschnitts sowie die Armaus-schnittstiefe können frei festgelegt wer-den, jedoch sollte man beim Vorderteil eine Mindesthöhe nicht unterschreiten. Es ist hilfreich, sich dabei an Brustlinie und Schulterpunkt zu orientieren sowie die Maße direkt am Körper auszuprobieren.

3. Wie schon beim Vorderteil orientiert man sich beim Rückenteil am Grundschnitt des Kleides. Form und Höhe des Rückenteils können dabei vom Vorderteil abweichen, allerdings sollte die Länge der Seitennaht, an der Vorder- und Rückenteil zusammen-gefügt werden, übereinstimmen.

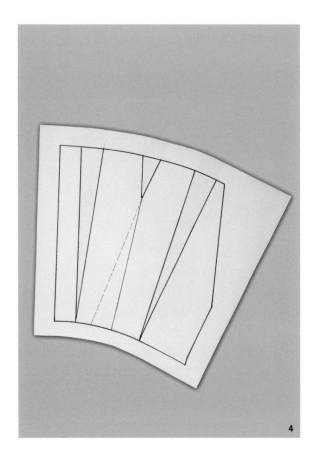

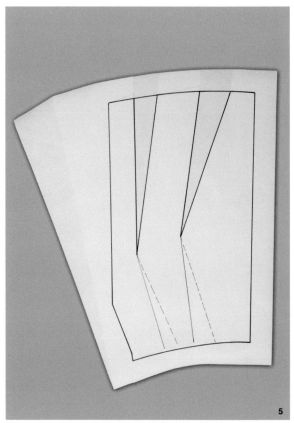

4

5

4. The drape gathered in the neckline also needs extra volume which is now added into the copied cut-out part so that this can be ruched later through the cord. You obtain the required fullness by cutting and opening the darts.

In the front part, bust and waist darts meet together in the bust apex. Here the waist dart can comfortably be shifted into the upper neckline edge: For this you cut open an edge of the bust dart, add in the waist dart and in this way obtain the required width in the neckline.

Subsequent to this, two cuts are made to the right and to the left of the bust dart to gain extra volume and the volume added in. The cut edges – i.e. waistline and neckline edge – must now be rounded off to smooth out the corners that have been formed.

5. In the back part the additional volume is gained by drawing guiding lines from the points of the darts to the upper neckline

4. Les plis retroussés nécessitent un volume supplémentaire, qui s'ajoute à la partie copiée du patron, afin de pouvoir ensuite les faire coulisser à l'aide du cordon. La largeur supplémentaire nécessaire est obtenue en coupant et en défaisant les pinces.

Dans la partie avant, la pince de la poitrine et la pince de la taille se trouvent sur la pointe de la poitrine. Ici, il est possible de déplacer aisément la pince de la taille jusqu'à l'extrémité supérieure de la coupe : il faut pour cela découper une partie de la pince de la poitrine, puis ajouter la pince de la taille pour obtenir la largeur nécessaire pour la coupe.

Deux coupes sont ensuite effectuées à gauche et à droite de la pince de la poitrine afin d'apporter plus de volume, et celui-ci sera ensuite froncé. Les bords de coupe, c'est-à-dire, la ligne de taille et l'extrémité de l'encolure, doivent alors être dessinées de manière arrondie, afin d'égaliser les angles.

4. Der im Ausschnitt geraffte Faltenwurf braucht zusätzliches Volumen, das nun in das herauskopierte Schnittteil einfügt wird, damit dieses später durch die Kordel gerüscht werden kann. Die benötigte Mehrweite erhält man durch Einschneiden und Aufdrehen der Abnäher.

Im Vorderteil treffen sich Brust- und Taillenabnäher in der Brustspitze. Hier kann der Taillenabnäher bequem in die obere Ausschnittkante verlegt werden: Man schneidet dazu einen Schenkel des Brustabnähers auf, legt den Taillenabnäher zu und erhält so die benötigte Weite im Ausschnitt.

Im Anschluss daran werden zur Gewinnung zusätzlichen Volumens zwei Einschnitte rechts und links vom Brustabnäher ausgeführt und das Volumen eingedreht. Die Schnittkanten – d.h. Taillenlinie und Ausschnittkante – müssen nun gerundet ausgezeichnet werden, um die entstandenen Ecken auszugleichen.

6

edge and indeed by dividing the neckline into three. These guiding lines are now cut open and the waist darts added i.e. dart edge stuck on dart edge. Thus the fullness in the neckline springs open; the missing paper is stuck underneath as also with the front part.

6. The ruches of the upper part obtain a soft fall with the fabric being on the bias. The shoulder band can be fastened with a bow.

5. Sur la partie arrière, nous obtenons plus de volume en traçant des lignes auxiliaires allant des pointes des pinces jusqu'à l'extrémité supérieure de l'encolure, et en divisant également en trois parties la ligne de l'encolure. Ces lignes auxiliaires doivent être coupées et ajoutées aux pinces de la taille, c'est-à-dire collées bout sur bout. La largeur supplémentaire de la coupe se forme alors peu à peu, et le papier qui manque est collé sous la partie avant.

6. Les volants plissés de la partie supérieure présentent une retombée plus souple grâce à la couture en diagonale. Le ruban sur les épaules se règle avec un cordon.

5. Im Rückenteil wird das zusätzliche Volumen gewonnen, indem von den Abnäherspitzen zur oberen Ausschnittkante Hilfslinien gezogen werden, und zwar durch eine Drittelung der Ausschnittslinie. Diese Hilfslinien werden nun aufgeschnitten und die Taillenabnäher zugelegt, d.h. Schenkel auf Schenkel geklebt. Dadurch springt die Mehrweite im Ausschnitt auf; das fehlende Papier wird wie auch beim Vorderteil darunter geklebt.

6. Die Rüschen des Oberteils erhalten durch den schrägen Fadenlauf einen weichen Fall. Das Schulterband kann durch eine Schleife reguliert werden.

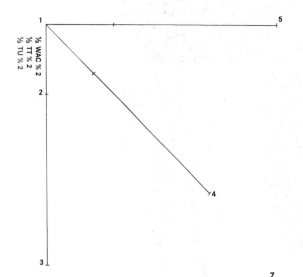

1/3 WAC % 2
1/3 TT % 2
1/3 TU % 2

1

2

3

5

4

7

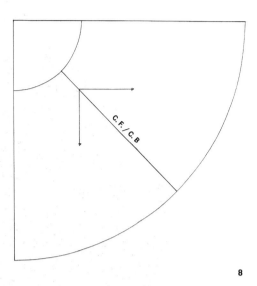

C. F. / C. B

8

7. The lower part of the dress is based on a flared skirt – a skirt pattern which is constructed on circular arcs. The upper circular arc is crucial for the width of the waist, the second for the width of the skirt hem. In the following example the construction of the semi-circular flared skirt is illustrated.

We begin with a long vertical line on which both a right angle as well as a 45 degree line is drawn at Point 1.

You obtain Point 2 by going out 1/3 of the waist circumference % 2 cm from Point 1 on both angle edges. With a waist circumference of 68 cm, this corresponds to a value of 20.66 cm. You go out the desired skirt length, here 50 cm, starting from Point 2 and in this way gain Point 3.

8. Starting from Point 1, two circular arcs are now drawn. If you work with a drawing to scale you use a compass, if on the other hand you start from the actual size, a tape measure or a part of string which can be held with a hand at the turning point

7. La partie inférieure de la robe consiste en une jupe à volants, un modèle fabriqué avec des arcs en cercle. L'arc en cercle supérieur est déterminant pour la largeur de la taille, et le deuxième arc, pour la largeur de l'extrémité de la jupe. La confection de la jupe de manière semi-circulaire est illustrée dans l'exemple suivant.

En commençant par une longue ligne verticale, il faut ensuite tracer, à partir du point 1, une ligne vers la droite et une ligne avec un angle de 45 degrés.

Le point 2 s'obtient en traçant 1/3 du tour de la taille % 2 cm à partir du point 1 dans les deux directions. Si le tour de taille est de 68 cm, la valeur correspondante est de 20,66 cm. La longueur de jupe souhaitée, ici 50 cm, est tracée à partir du point 2 pour créer le point 3.

8. Dessiner ensuite deux arcs en cercle en partant du point 1. Si le travail est réalisé avec des dessins à l'échelle, un compas est alors nécessaire, mais si au contraire les dimensions utilisées sont celles d'ori-

7. Der untere Teil des Kleides basiert auf einem Glockenrock – ein Rockmodell, das auf Kreisbögen konstruiert wird. Der obere Kreisbogen ist ausschlaggebend für die Taillenweite, der zweite Bogen für die Saumweite des Rocks. Im folgenden Beispiel wird die Konstruktion des halbkreisrunden Glockenrocks illustriert.

Begonnen wird mit einer langen senkrechten Linie, auf der bei Punkt 1 sowohl eine Winkellinie nach rechts als auch eine 45-Grad-Linie gezogen werden.

Punkt 2 erhält man, indem 1/3 des Taillenumfangs % 2 cm vom Punkt 1 aus auf beiden Schenkeln abgetragen werden. Bei einem Taillenumfang von 68 cm entspricht das einem Wert von 20,66 cm. Die gewünschte Rocklänge, hier 50 cm, trägt man vom Punkt 2 ausgehend ab und gewinnt so Punkt 3.

8. Vom Punkt 1 ausgehend, werden nun zwei Kreisbögen gezogen. Wenn man mit einer Maßstabszeichnung arbeitet, benutzt man einen Zirkel, geht man hingegen

whilst the other draws the circular arc are the most suitable. The drawing formed in this way presents half of the skirt and is to be used both for the front and also the back part, since both parts are identical. The line in Point 4 is thus the centre front and centre back. The line in Point 5 and the line in Point 3 form both side seams and also the run of the grain. The centre front and centre back are as a result on the bias.

9. The folds fall softly and regularly because of the bias and the generous volume. The bias however has an adverse effect in the waist area, since the fabric gently spreads. It is therefore important to check the waist circumference before sewing together the upper and lower part and to fix the desired measurement through a firm tape or band.

gine, il est préférable d'utiliser un mètre à ruban ou un bout de cordon, qui est maintenu avec une main au point de rotation pendant que l'autre main dessine l'arc en cercle. Le croquis tracé représente la moitié de la jupe et peut être utilisé aussi bien pour la partie avant que la partie arrière, puisque les deux sont identiques. La ligne du point 4 constitue donc le milieu avant et du dos. La ligne du point 5 et la ligne du point 3 constituent la couture latérale et le guide-fil. Par conséquent, les milieus avant et du dos se recoupent sur le guide-fil en diagonale.

9. Les plis retombent de manière souple et régulière grâce au volume important et à la couture en diagonale. Cela présente un inconvénient puisque le fil en diagonale est visible dans la zone de la taille, du fait que le tissu s'étire un peu. Il est pour cela important, avant de coudre la partie supérieure sur la partie inférieure, de vérifier le tour de taille et définir la mesure souhaitée avec un ruban fixe.

von der Originalgröße aus, eigenen sich am besten ein Maßband oder ein Stück Schnur, die mit einer Hand am Drehpunkt gehalten wird, während die andere den Kreisbogen zieht. Die so entstandene Zeichnung stellt die Hälfte des Rockes dar und ist sowohl für das Vorder- als auch für das Rückenteil zu verwenden, da beide Teile identisch sind. Die Linie in Punkt 4 ist somit die Vordere und Hintere Mitte. Die Linie in Punkt 5 und die Linie in Punkt 3 bilden sowohl die Seitennähte als auch die Fadenläufe. Die Vordere und Hintere Mitte befinden sich demzufolge im schrägen Fadenlauf.

9. Die Falten fallen durch den schrägen Fadenlauf und das großzügige Volumen weich und regelmäßig. Nachteilig wirkt sich der schräge Fadenlauf jedoch im Taillenbereich aus, da sich der Stoff leicht dehnt. Es ist daher wichtig, vor dem Zusammennähen des Ober- und Unterteils den Taillenumfang zu überprüfen und das gewünschte Maß durch ein festes Band oder Bund zu fixieren.

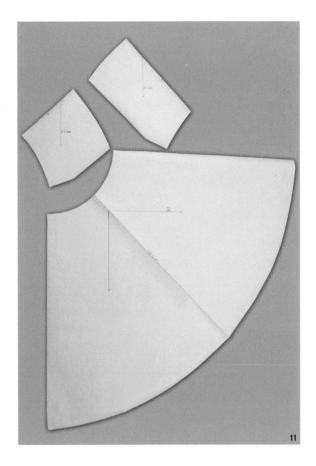

10. You can use the tape measure or simply a part of string as an aid for drawing the large circular arcs.

11. The completed cut-out parts of the upper part are cut on the bias of the fabric. The skirt part on the other hand is laid on the grain so as to place the centre front and centre back on the bias – i.e. in the 45 degree angle.

12. Through the combination of gathered and freely-swinging folds, there emerges here a visual effect of particular attractiveness.

10. Pour dessiner le grand arc en cercle, il est possible de s'aider d'un mètre à ruban ou d'un bout de ficelle.

11. Les pièces terminées de la partie supérieure sont découpées sur le tissu en diagonale par rapport au fil. En revanche, la pièce de la jupe est mise en place en suivant le fil, afin d'obtenir le milieu avant et du dos en position oblique, c'est-à-dire, avec un angle de 45 degrés.

12. La combinaison entre les plis à volants et les fronces donne un bel effet visuel et un certain charme.

10. Als Hilfsmittel für das Zeichnen der großen Kreisbögen kann man das Maßband oder einfach ein Stück Schnur verwenden.

11. Die fertigen Schnittteile des Oberteils werden auf dem Stoff im schrägen Fadenlauf zugeschnitten. Das Rockteil wird demgegenüber im Fadenlauf aufgelegt, um dadurch die Vordere und Hintere Mitte schräg – also im 45-Grad-Winkel – zu platzieren.

12. Durch die Kombination von gerafften und freischwingenden Falten entsteht hier ein visueller Effekt von besonderem Reiz.

Dress with oval outline
Robe à silhouette ovale
Kleid mit ovaler Silhouette

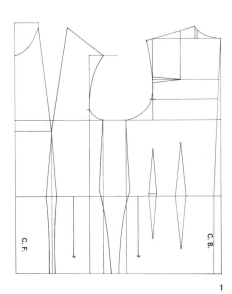

C. F.

C. B.

1

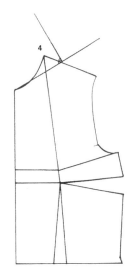

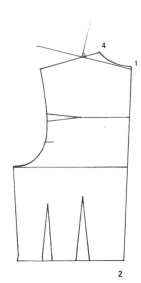

2

1. In contrast to the previous pattern, this dress has no falling, soft lines, but rather a static shape. The oval outline, the cut-out stand-up collar, the graphically slanting darts and the seamless small sleeves which cover the shoulders only slightly, lend to this pattern a very individual note.

2. Before you can begin with the actual work on the stand-up collar, you must first of all deepen the neckline. For this purpose you go down respectively 1 cm at the centre back and 4 cm at the shoulder seam from the basic pattern. The newly

1. Contrairement au modèle précédent, cette robe ne présente pas de lignes à retombée souple, mais plutôt une forme statique. La silhouette ovale, le col élevé, les pinces obliques et les petites manches sans coutures, qui recouvrent à peine les épaules, donnent au modèle un style très personnel.

2. Avant de pouvoir commencer à travailler sur le col élevé, il faut tout d'abord ouvrir l'orifice de la tête. Il faut pour cela commencer sur le modèle de base en descendant de 1 cm sur le milieu du dos et

1. Im Gegensatz zum vorhergehenden Modell besitzt dieses Kleid keine fallenden weichen Linien, sondern eine statische Form. Die ovale Silhouette, der angeschnittene Stehkragen, die graphisch schrägen Abnäher und die nahtlosen kleinen Ärmel, die die Schultern nur leicht bedecken, verleihen dem Modell eine sehr individuelle Note.

2. Bevor mit der eigentlichen Arbeit am Stehkragen begonnen werden kann, muss zuerst das Halsloch vertieft werden. Zu diesem Zweck geht man vom Grundmo-

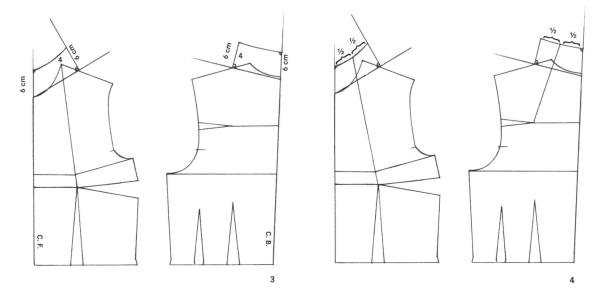

3

4

formed points are linked by a straight line which serves at the same time as the fixing-line for the angle line upwards.

3. In the next step, you lengthen the line of the centre front and centre back upwards and cut it off at 6 cm as with the angle line you have just constructed. You draw in the new collar line with a curve ruler.

4. Then on the new collar edge the respective centre of each collar quarter is ascertained and a line drawn to the point of the dart. In this way the cutting-lines and dart edges are revealed.

5. For aesthetic reasons, you shift the bust darts of the front part and the shoulder darts of the back part located in the armhole into the collar area. As indicated in drawing 5, to achieve this, the cutting lines are cut into and the original darts added such that the dart content passes into the new line. In this way, the collar springs apart. The newly formed areas are spliced with paper.

6. In the collar and bust area you need additional leeway to achieve a more rounded collar. You achieve this if the dart depths are each reduced 1 cm per side, you add therefore 1 cm per side.

de 4 cm sur la couture de l'épaule. Les nouveaux points obtenus sont reliés par une ligne droite, qui sert également de ligne auxiliaire pour la ligne angulaire vers le haut.

3. Il faut ensuite prolonger la ligne du milieu avant et du dos vers le haut, en ajoutant 6 cm à cette ligne ainsi qu'à la ligne droite angulaire. La nouvelle ligne du col doit être dessinée avec un patron à courbes.

4. Puis, calculer le milieu du quart de col sur le nouveau bord du col et tracer une ligne jusqu'à l'extrémité de la pince. Les lignes de coupe et les côtés des pinces sont ainsi créés.

5. Pour des raisons esthétiques, la pince de la poitrine sur la partie avant et la pince de l'épaule, située dans l'orifice du bras sur la partie arrière, sont déplacées vers la zone du col. Tel que l'illustre la figure 5, les lignes de coupe sont découpées et les pinces d'xorigine sont mises en place, de sorte que celles-ci deviennent la nouvelle ligne. Ainsi, l'élaboration du col se poursuit. Les nouvelles surfaces créées sont collées avec du papier.

dell an der Hinteren Mitte 1 cm und an der Schulternaht jeweils 4 cm nach unten. Die neu entstandenen Punkte werden mit einer Geraden verbunden, die zugleich als Anlagelinie für die Winkellinie nach oben dient.

3. Im nächsten Schritt verlängert man die Linie der Vorderen und Hinteren Mitte nach oben und trägt auf dieser wie auch auf der gerade konstruierten Winkellinie 6 cm ab. Mit einem Kurvenlineal zeichnet man die neue Kragenlinie ein.

4. Dann wird auf der neuen Kragenkante die jeweilige Mitte des Kragenviertels ermittelt und eine Linie zur Abnäherspitze gezogen. So entstehen die Einschneidelinien bzw. die Abnäherschenkel.

5. Aus ästhetischen Gründen verlegt man den Brustabnäher des Vorderteils und den sich im Armloch befindenden Schulterabnäher des Rückenteils in den Kragenbereich. Wie in Zeichnung 5 abgebildet, werden zu diesem Zweck die Einschneidelinien eingeschnitten und die ursprünglichen Abnäher zugelegt, sodass der Abnäherinhalt in die neue Linie übergeht. Auf diese Weise springt der Kragen auseinander. Die neu entstandenen Bereiche werden mit Papier unterklebt.

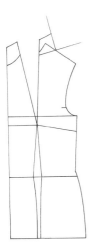
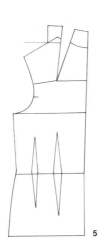

5

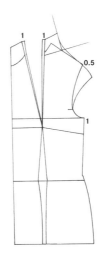
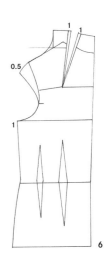

6

The pattern sleeves are sketched at the armhole. A line close to the body line is created by drawing in the shoulder point slightly rounded (0.5 cm), for this however the armhole is deepened by 1 cm such that it is in no way too narrow under the arm.

7-8. The shoulder lines must have the same length and shape to be able to sew together front and back part without problem. The simplest way of accomplishing this is by measuring the shoulder lines or even better making a part stencil of the back part which is then transferred to the front part. The best way of ensuring the dress can be put on and taken off comfortably is by using a covered zip in the left shoulder seam.

9. The oval outline of the dress emerges through an optional lengthening of the basic pattern and drawing in a rounded side seam. The waist darts are therefore ignored since the dress does not fit in a figure-hugging way at the waist.

6. Une marge supplémentaire doit être ajoutée dans la zone du col et de la poitrine afin de pouvoir arrondir correctement le col. Il faut pour cela réduire de 1 cm la profondeur de la pince d'un côté et rajouter 1 cm de l'autre.
Les manches coupées doivent être ébauchées dans l'orifice du bras. Il est possible de créer une ligne ajustée au corps en dessinant la pointe de l'épaule avec une légère courbure (0,5 cm), et en approfondissant de 1 cm dans l'orifice du bras afin que le dessous de bras ne soit pas trop serré.

7-8. Les lignes des épaules doivent avoir la même longueur et la même forme, afin de pouvoir relier les parties avant et arrière sans trop de problème. Le plus simple est de prendre des mesures des lignes des épaules ou, encore mieux, d'élaborer un patron gradué de la partie arrière, qui ensuite est reporté sur la partie avant. Cette robe, facile à mettre et à enlever, peut être complétée par une fermeture éclair à coutures cachées du côté gauche.

6. Im Kragen- und Brustbereich braucht man noch zusätzlichen Spielraum, um einen runderen Stand des Kragens zu erzielen. Das erreicht man, wenn die Abnähertiefe um jeweils 1 cm pro Seite verringert wird, man fügt also pro Seite 1 cm hinzu. Die angeschnittenen Ärmel werden am Armloch skizziert. Eine körpernahe Linie lässt sich kreieren, indem die Schulterspitze leicht abgerundet eingezeichnet wird (0,5 cm), dafür aber das Armloch um 1 cm vertieft wird, sodass es unter dem Arm auf keinen Fall zu eng wird.

7-8. Die Schulterlinien müssen die gleiche Länge und Form aufweisen, um Vorder- und Rückenteil problemlos zusammenfügen zu können. Am einfachsten lässt sich dies bewerkstelligen, indem man die Schulterlinien ausmisst, oder besser noch eine Teilschablone des Rückenteils anfertigt, die dann auf das Vorderteil übertragen wird. Das bequeme An- und Ausziehen des Kleides kann man am besten erreichen durch einen nahtverdeckten Reißverschluss in der linken Schulternaht.

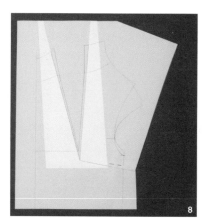

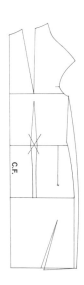

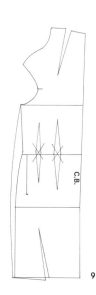

C.F.

C.B.

7

8

9

For reasons of visual symmetry, darts can also be laid in the hem, if desired. They also strengthen the balloon-shaped outline of the dress. The length and position of the darts are decided according to each individual design.

It is worth observing that both dart edges must always be measured and adjusted so that the darts can be sewn without problem. The edge next to the center is crucial as it defines the length. In a crooked position, the dart edge can run out over the original hem. The corner of the side seam must be drawn in again on a right angle.

9. La silhouette ovale de la robe est obtenue en prolongeant le patron de base autant que souhaité et en traçant une couture latérale arrondie. Les pinces de la taille ne sont pas prises en compte, étant donné que la robe n'est pas coupée sur mesure.

Pour des raisons de symétrie visuelle, il est aussi possible de rajouter des pinces sur le bord. Ces pinces font ressortir le profil arrondi de la robe. La longueur et la position des pinces peuvent être déterminées librement.

Il convient de rappeler que les deux côtés des pinces doivent toujours être comparés et ajustés, pour éviter tout problème au moment de coudre les pinces. Dans ce cas précis, le côté proche du centre s'avère déterminant, puisqu'il définit la longueur. En raison de sa position en diagonale, le côté déplacé peut dépasser sur le bord d'origine. L'angle de la couture latérale doit être à nouveau marqué en angle droit.

9. Die ovale Silhouette des Kleides entsteht durch eine beliebige Verlängerung des Grundschnitts und eine eingezeichnete gerundete Seitennaht. Die Taillenabnäher werden deshalb ignoriert, da das Kleid in der Taille nicht figurbetont anliegt.

Aus Gründen der optischen Symmetrie können, wenn gewünscht, in den Saum ebenfalls Abnäher gelegt werden. Sie verstärken zusätzlich die ballonförmige Silhouette des Kleides. Länge und Lage der Abnäher werden je nach Entwurf festgelegt.

Es gilt zu beachten, dass die beiden Abnäherschenkel immer nachgemessen und angeglichen werden müssen, damit die Abnäher problemlos genäht werden können. Maßgebend ist dabei der zur jeweiligen Mitte hin liegende Schenkel, er gibt die Länge vor. Durch die schräge Lage kann der übertragene Schenkel über den ursprünglichen Saum hinaus reichen. Die Ecke der Seitennaht muss wieder rechtwinklig ausgezeichnet werden.

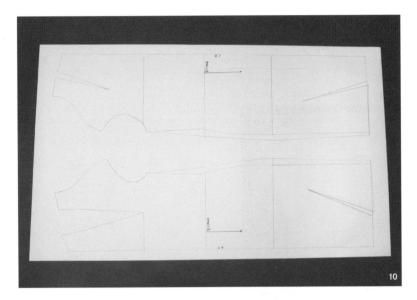

10

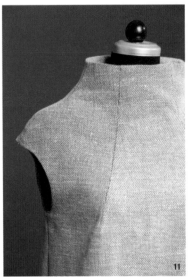

11

10. The completed pattern parts: The centre front and centre back of this pattern are on the fold.

11. The pattern sleeves and the stand-up collar give the pattern a particular note. For this you need a fabric with a certain class. It is probably helpful to strengthen both the collar-shoulder area as well as the hem with inter-linings.

10. Les pièces de coupe terminées : les milieus avant et du dos de ce modèle sont séparées.

11. Les manches découpées ainsi que le col de la robe élevé, soulevé et écarté du cou, donnent une touche particulière au modèle. Le tissu utilisé doit pour cela présenter une certaine texture. Il peut s'avérer utile de renforcer la zone du col et des épaules, ainsi que le bord de la robe avec une doublure.

10. Die fertigen Schnittteile: Vordere und Hintere Mitte dieses Modells liegen im Bruch.

11. Die angeschnittenen Ärmel und der halsferne Stehkragen geben dem Modell eine besondere Note. Dazu benötigt man einen Stoff mit einem gewissen Stand. Eventuell ist es hilfreich, sowohl den Kragen-Schulterbereich als auch den Saum mit Einlagen zu verstärken.

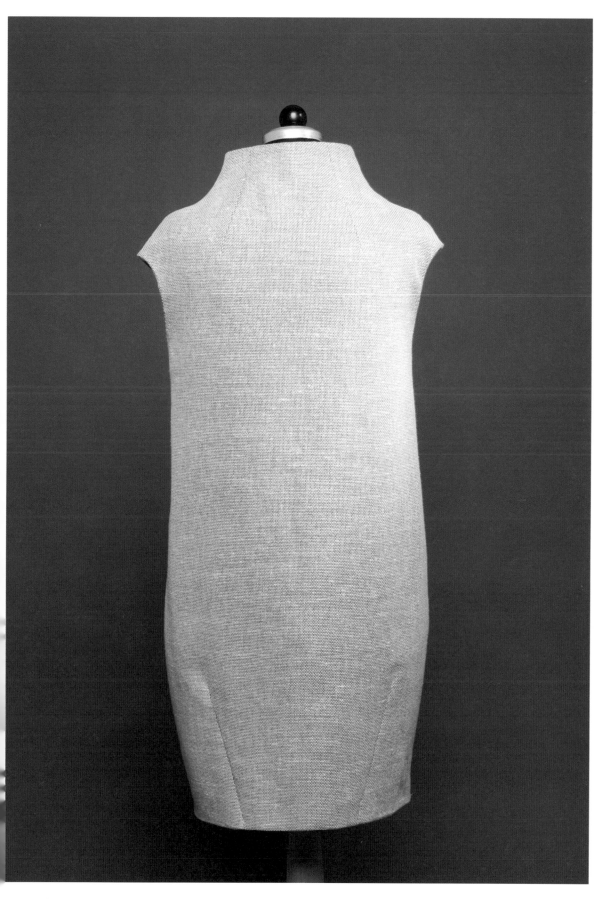

Jacket with flounce collar and raglan sleeve
Veste à col volanté et manche raglan
Jacke mit Volantkragen und Raglanärmel

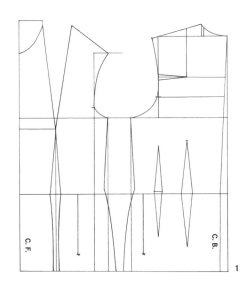

1. Since this jacket pattern sits relatively close on the shoulder and waist, the basic cut-out for dresses is also used as a basis here. The necessary width is achieved through gathering. The special shape of the flounce collar can also be highlighted by using two different fabrics. A raglan sleeve is added here as an extension of the basic cut-out.

1. Étant donné que ce modèle de veste est relativement serré au niveau des épaules et de la taille, le patron de base de robe est également utilisé ici comme support. La largeur nécessaire sera obtenue par juxtapositions. La forme particulière du col volanté peut être mise en valeur en employant deux tissus différents. Une manche raglan vient s'ajouter pour agrandir le patron de base.

1. Da dieses Jackenmodell relativ eng an Schulter und Taille sitzt, wird auch hier der Kleidergrundschnitt als Basis verwendet. Die nötige Weite wird durch Reihung erzielt. Die besondere Form des Volantkragens kann zusätzlich durch die Verwendung zweier verschiedener Stoffe hervorgehoben werden. Als Erweiterung des Grundschnittes wird hier ein Raglanärmel eingefügt.

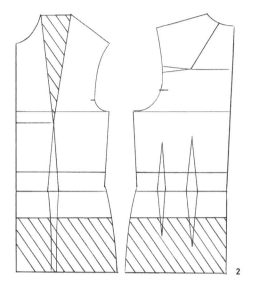

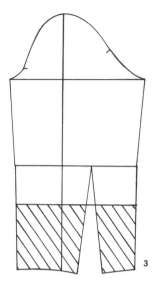

2. At the beginning you draw in the pattern lines of the waist yoke. Here, the lines run approximately 5 cm over the waist and 7 cm underneath. The area lying underneath falls away in the case of this jacket which sits in the waist. The darts are added in the upper jacket parts; the front one is laid into the waist to produce an expanse of gathers, the back as visual detail into the neckline.

3. The sleeve, which is set in according to the "raglan system", is made from the sleeve basic pattern from page 60. Initially you extend the line from the highest point of the sleeve straight to the hem; that produces the later join. You then shorten the sleeve to the desired length, here approx. 42 cm.

2. Pour commencer, dessiner les lignes de base du tour de taille. Les lignes passent ici à environ 5 cm au-dessus de la taille et 7 cm en dessous. La zone située dans la moitié inférieure est omise sur cette veste ajustée à la taille. Préparer la disposition des pinces sur la partie supérieure de la veste. La pince avant est placée de manière à agrandir la veste, alors que celle du dos est utilisée comme un détail visuel dans l'orifice du col.

3. La manche, de type raglan, sera confectionnée avec le patron de base de manche de la page 60. La ligne est ensuite prolongée du point le plus élevé de la manche jusqu'à l'ourlet. Cette opération permet d'obtenir la ligne de division arrière. Les manches sont alors raccourcies à la longueur souhaitée. Dans ce cas, environ 42 cm.

2. Zu Beginn zeichnet man die Modelllinien der Taillenpasse ein. Hier verlaufen die Linien etwa 5 cm über der Taille und 7 cm darunter. Der unterhalb liegende Bereich fällt bei dieser in der Taille sitzenden Jacke weg. Das Zulegen der Abnäher in den oberen Jackenteilen wird vorbereitet; der Vordere wird als Reihweite in die Taille gelegt, der Hintere als optisches Detail ins Halsloch.

3. Der Ärmel, der nach dem „Raglansystem" angelegt wird, wird mit dem Ärmelgrundschnitt von Seite 60 hergestellt. Zunächst verlängert man die Linie vom höchsten Punkt des Ärmels gerade bis zum Saum; das ergibt die spätere Teilungslinie. Man kürzt dann den Ärmel auf die gewünschte Länge, hier ca. 42 cm.

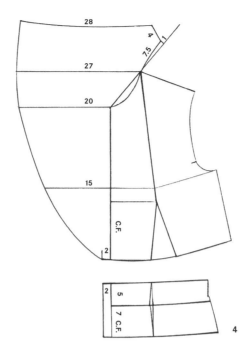

4. Afterwards the yokes are separated from the top parts of the jacket; the bust darts are laid into the waist.

You obtain the cut-out collar on the front part if you draw a line from the neck outline centre to the neckline apex and beyond. From the neckline apex, you go out by the measured amount of the rear neckline, angle *1 cm* upwards and draw the outline of the collar slightly rounded.

Then you establish the collar width and height according to free measurement. The centimeters specified are only a recommendation; the collar can of course be designed with more volume as well as less. It is however important that the collar runs in again below, and indeed at the joining *approx. 1.5 to 2 cm* before the centre front.

Through the darts laid in the waist, the upper part obtains the fullness which is then gathered in and caught in to the waist yoke. This can be over the entire width or only concentrated on a certain length.

The join at the yoke is also specified and the darts added in the cut-out. The width

4. Puis, les ceintures sont détachées de la partie supérieure de la veste. La pince de poitrine sera placée sur la taille.

Le col raccourci dans sa partie avant est obtenu en dessinant une ligne allant de la coupe du col jusqu'à l'extrémité de l'orifice du col, d'où elle est prolongée. À partir de l'extrémité de l'orifice du col, équilibrer la longueur mesurée de l'orifice du col dans le dos, plier de *1 cm* vers le haut et dessiner la ligne de prolongement du col légèrement arrondie.

La hauteur et la largeur du col sont alors établies librement. Les centimètres mentionnés ici sont donnés à titre indicatif. Le col peut bien entendu être dessiné plus volumineux ou plus fin. Cependant, il est important que le col se rétrécisse à nouveau au point de jonction *entre 1,5 y 2 cm environ* de milieu avant.

Les pinces de la taille donnent plus d'ampleur à la partie supérieure, et celle-ci sera ajustée par la suite à la ceinture. La jonction peut être réalisée sur toute la largeur de la pièce ou se concentrer sur un segment concret.

4. Anschließend werden die Passen von den oberen Jackenteilen getrennt; der Brustabnäher wird in die Taille gelegt.

Den an das Vorderteil angeschnittenen Kragen erhält man, wenn man eine Linie vom Halsausschnitt zur Halslochspitze und darüber hinaus zieht. Ab der Halslochspitze trägt man den ausgemessenen Betrag des hinteren Halslochs ab, winkelt *1 cm* nach oben und zeichnet die Ansatzlinie des Kragens leicht gerundet aus.

Dann legt man die Kragenbreite und -höhe nach freiem Ermessen fest. Die angegebenen Zentimeter sind nur eine Empfehlung, der Kragen kann natürlich sowohl voluminöser als auch schmaler gestaltet werden. Wichtig jedoch ist, dass der Kragen unten wieder einläuft, und zwar am Übertritt *ca. 1,5 bis 2 cm* vor der Vorderen Mitte.

Durch den in die Taille gelegten Abnäher erhält das Oberteil die Mehrweite, die dann eingereiht und an der Taillenpasse gefasst wird. Die Fassung kann über die gesamte Breite erfolgen oder sich nur auf eine bestimmte Strecke konzentrieren.

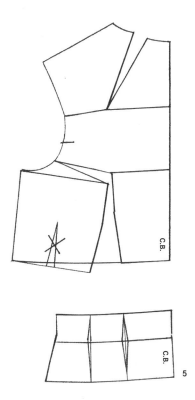

C.B.

C.B.

5

remaining in the dart centre can be taken away at the side seam after trying on.

5. At the back part, the desired expanse of gathers is effected by cutting into and opening up the dart at the armhole. The gap formed is spliced. If the gathers are later caught in at the waist yoke, the armhole finds itself in its original position again. The size of the opening can be determined according to taste or corresponding to the front part. The second dart is not sewn and also gives width.
Through the opening a shifting of the parts takes places at the hemline of the upper part which must be evened round slightly again.
The darts are added at the yoke as with the front part. The upper and lower back part are laid with the centre back on the fold.

La jonction à la ceinture sera fixée de la même manière et les pinces seront incluses dans la coupe. La largeur restante au centre de la pince pourra être éliminée après l'essayage au niveau de la couture latérale.

5. La largeur souhaitée de l'élargissement s'effectue dans le dos et est obtenue en coupant et en orientant les pinces vers le poignet. L'espace obtenu sera collé. Lorsque par la suite l'élargissement sera fixé à la ceinture, le poignet retournera dans sa position d'origine. La taille de l'orifice peut être ajustée selon les goûts ou en l'adaptant à la partie avant La deuxième pince ne sera pas cousue et donnera ainsi à la pièce davantage d'ampleur
L'ouverture entraîne un déplacement des pièces sur la ligne de l'ourlet de la partie supérieure. Cette ouverture devra de nouveau être arrondie et égalisée.
De même que sur la partie avant, les pinces seront placées au niveau de la ceinture. Les parties supérieure et inférieure du dos seront situées au niveau de l'ouverture du milieu du dos.

Der Übertritt an der Passe wird ebenfalls angegeben und der Abnäher im Schnitt zugelegt. Die in der Abnähermitte übrig bleibende Weite kann nach der Anprobe an der Seitennaht weggenommen werden.

5. Am Rückenteil entsteht die gewünschte Reihweite durch Einschneiden und Aufdrehen des Abnähers zum Armloch. Der entstandene Spalt wird unterklebt. Wenn die Reihung später an der Taillenpasse gefasst wird, findet das Armloch wieder in seine ursprüngliche Position zurück. Die Größe der Öffnung kann je nach Geschmack oder korrespondierend zum Vorderteil bestimmt werden. Der zweite Abnäher wird nicht genäht und gibt zusätzlich Weite.
Durch die Öffnung findet an der Saumlinie des Oberteils eine Verschiebung der Teile statt, die wieder leicht gerundet ausgeglichen werden muss.
An der Passe werden wie auch schon beim Vorderteil die Abnäher zugelegt. Oberes und unteres Rückenteil werden in der hinteren Mitte in den Bruch gelegt.

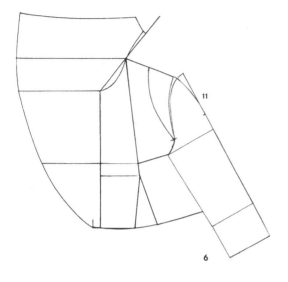

6

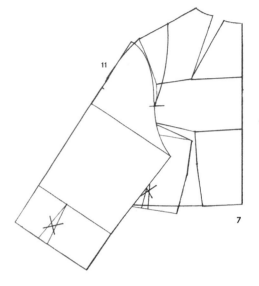

11

7

6. Before the sleeve is cut apart along the already drawn centre line, *11 cm* however must initially be drawn from above. This marker point later serves for comparing the length of the shoulder seams.

At the front part the left sleeve part is then fitted, and indeed in such a way that both sleeve inset markers lie on top of each other. An interval of *1 cm* is to be observed at the end of the shoulder line; this is the additional length which is needed for the shoulder pad.

Now a separation seam must be drawn in, since the sleeve covers a part of the jacket part and a combined cut through that is not possible.

This separation seam can run in freely chosen curve from any point of the neckline or the shoulder seam to the sleeve inset marker. Here, both the cut-out parts separate and the seam ends in the respective sleeve outline curves of the jacket part and the sleeve part.

6. Avant de couper la manche le long de la ligne centrale déjà tracée, il faudra dessiner ensuite *11 cm* à partir de la partie supérieure. Ce point de référence permettra par la suite d'égaliser la longueur des coutures au niveau des épaules.

Il faudra alors placer la pièce de la manche gauche sur la partie avant de sorte que les motifs des deux manches se superposent. Il faudra respecter une distance de *1 cm* à l'extrémité de la ligne de l'épaule. Cette ligne correspond à la longueur supplémentaire nécessaire à la mise en place de l'épaulette.

Il faudra entre temps dessiner une couture de séparation, étant donné que la manche recouvre une partie de la veste et qu'il est impossible d'effectuer une coupe commune au travers de celle-ci.

Cette couture de séparation pourra être réalisée suivant la courbure souhaitée à partir d'un point quelconque de l'orifice du col ou de la couture de l'épaule jusqu'aux pièces insérées des manches. Dans ce cas, les deux parties de la coupe sont séparées et la couture se termine au niveau des courbures de coupe des manches de la veste et de la manche.

6. Bevor der Ärmel entlang der bereits gezogenen Mittellinie auseinander geschnitten wird, müssen allerdings zunächst *11 cm* von oben abgezeichnet werden. Dieser Anhaltspunkt dient später dazu, die Länge der Schulternähte vergleichen zu können.

Am Vorderteil wird dann der linke Ärmelteil aufgelegt, und zwar so, dass die beiden Ärmeleinsatzzeichen übereinander liegen. Ein Abstand von *1 cm* ist am Ende der Schulterlinie zu beachten; dies ist die Mehrlänge, die für das Schulterpolster gebraucht wird.

Nun muss eine Abtrennungsnaht eingezeichnet werden, da ja der Ärmel ein Stück des Jackenteils abdeckt und ein gemeinsamer Zuschnitt dadurch nicht möglich ist.

Diese Abtrennungsnaht kann in frei gewählter Rundung von einem beliebigen Punkt des Halslochs oder der Schulternaht aus hin zum Ärmeleinsatzzeichen führen. Hier trennen sich die beiden Schnittteile und die Naht endet in den jeweiligen Ärmelausschnittrundungen des Jackenteils und des Ärmelteils.

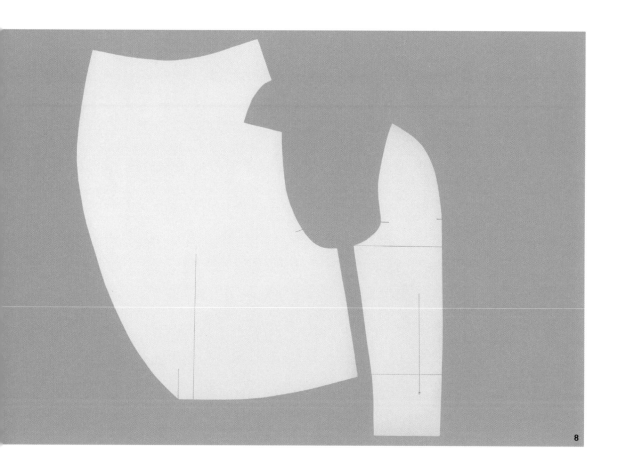

. The same steps are repeated on the
ack part with the right sleeve part. Here
gain, the sleeve inset markers must also
e laid over each other. The shoulder seam
f the back part should be measured again
efore affixing. The length of the shoulder
eam should correspond with the length
f the corresponding rear shoulder seam
lus a fullness of 0.6 cm) up to the 11-
entimeter point (see above) so that the
arts can be linked with each other.
he dart of the sleeve hem can be ignored
ith this pattern since the sleeve runs
traight. If however the sleeve hem is too
ide, the excess volume can be taken
way at the side seam.

. The photo shows the cut-out drawing
or the sleeve outline after the separation
long the new line. The shape of the line
an be done using your own measure-
ent, it must however be run through the
eeve inset marker and the shoulder lines
f the front and back part must have the
ame length.

7. Les mêmes étapes seront répétées sur
la partie arrière avec la pièce de la manche
droite. Dans ce cas, il faudra également
superposer les motifs des deux manches.
La couture de l'épaule de la pièce arrière
devra être mesurée avant de coller. La longueur de la couture de l'épaule de la partie
avant devra coïncider jusqu'au point des
11 centimètres (voir ci-dessus) de la couture correspondante de l'épaule au niveau
du dos (plus un espace supplémentaire de
0,6 cm), de sorte que les deux pièces puis-
sent être jointes entre elles.
La pince de l'ourlet de la manche peut ne
pas être prise en compte sur ce modèle
puisque la manche est droite. Si malgré
cela, l'ourlet de la manche est trop large,
le volume en trop pourra être éliminé sur
la couture latérale.

8. La photographie montre le dessin de la
coupe de la disposition des manches suite
à la séparation le long de la nouvelle ligne.
La forme de la ligne pourra être réalisée librement. Elle devra cependant passer par
les motifs des manches, et les lignes des
épaules avant et du dos devront être de la
même longueur.

7. Am Rückenteil werden die gleichen
Schritte mit dem rechten Ärmelteil wieder-
holt. Auch hier müssen die Ärmeleinsatzzeichen wieder übereinander liegen. Die
Schulternaht des Rückenteils sollte vor
dem Aufkleben nachgemessen werden.
Die Länge der Schulternaht des Vorderteils sollte dabei bis zum 11-Zentimeter-
Punkt (s. o.) mit der Länge der entsprechenden hinteren Schulternaht (plus einer
Mehrweite von 0,6 cm) übereinstimmen,
sodass beide Teile miteinander verbunden
werden können.
Der Ärmelsaumabnäher kann bei diesem
Modell ignoriert werden, da der Ärmel gerade verläuft. Ist der Ärmelsaum dennoch
zu weit, kann das überschüssige Volumen
an der Seitennaht weggenommen werden.

8. Das Foto zeigt die Schnittzeichnung für
die Ärmelanlage nach der Trennung entlang der neuen Linie. Die Form der Linie
kann nach eigenem Ermessen vorgenommen werden, sie muss allerdings durch
das Ärmeleinsatzzeichen führen und die
Schulterlinien von Vorder- und Rückteil
müssen die gleiche Länge aufweisen.

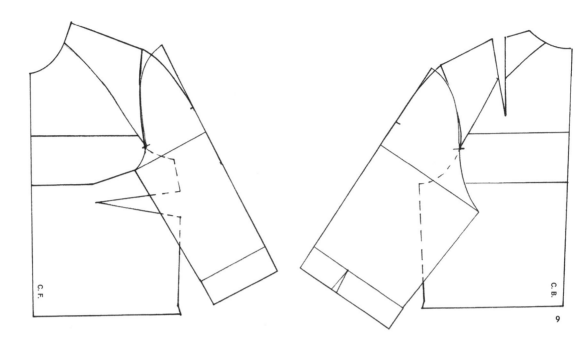

C. F.

C. B.

9

9. In principle you must ensure with the outline of raglan sleeves that the sleeve inset marker of sleeve and torso part always lie over each other congruently. The back part is always aimed at the front part; the shoulder seams of the sleeve must therefore have the same length. Moreover, an interval of *approx. 1 to 1.5 cm* on the shoulder must remain for the shoulder pad.

The line of the raglan separation on the other hand can be freely drawn. The position is decided by the desired design and can reach from the neckline via the shoulder or from the centre front via the sleeve insertion point to the side seam. Afterwards, the overlapping parts are copied out. The outlines here illustrate for example the separation of the raglan sleeve if you start from the neckline.

10. The parts ready for the cut-out in overview: the front and back sleeve part, front and back upper jacket part, front and back yoke. A little pocket can be drawn into the front yoke as an additional detail.

9. Lors de la mise en place des manches raglan, il faudra essentiellement tenir compte du fait que les motifs des manches et du torse doivent toujours se superposer de manière logique. La pièce de l'épaule est toujours orientée vers la partie avant et les coutures des épaules des manches devront donc être de la même longueur. De plus, il faudra laisser une distance comprise *entre 1 et 1,5 cm environ* sur les épaules pour les épaulettes.

En revanche, il ne sera pas nécessaire de modifier la ligne de séparation de la manche raglan. La position est choisie en fonction du dessin souhaité et peut aller de l'orifice du col au-dessus de l'épaule ou du milieu avant au-dessus du point de jonction de la manche jusqu'à la couture latérale. Les pièces qui seront rabattues seront ensuite copiées. Les croquis présentés ici illustrent en guise d'exemple la séparation de la manche raglan, à partir de l'orifice du col.

10. Vue panoramique des pièces terminées : Manche avant et dos, partie supérieure avant et dos de la veste, ceinture

9. Grundsätzlich ist bei der Anlage vo Raglanärmeln zu beachten, dass die Ä meleinsatzzeichen von Ärmel und Rump teil stets deckungsgleich übereinande liegen. Das Rückenteil richtet sich dabe immer nach dem Vorderteil, die Schulter nähte des Ärmels müssen also die gleich Länge aufweisen. Des Weiteren muss fü die Schulterpolster ein Abstand von ca 1 bis 1,5 cm an der Schulter vorbehalte bleiben.

Die Linie der Raglanabtrennung demge genüber kann frei gezogen werden. Di Position richtet sich nach dem gewünsch ten Design und kann vom Halsloch übe die Schulter oder von der Vorderen Mitt über den Ärmeleinsatzpunkt bis hin zu Seitennaht reichen. Danach werden di überlappenden Teile herauskopiert. Di Skizzen hier illustrieren beispielhaft di Abtrennung des Raglanärmels, wenn ma vom Halsloch ausgeht.

10. Die schnittfertigen Teile im Überblic vorderes und hinteres Ärmelteil, vordere und hinteres Jackenoberteil, vordere un hintere Passe. Als zusätzliches Detail kar

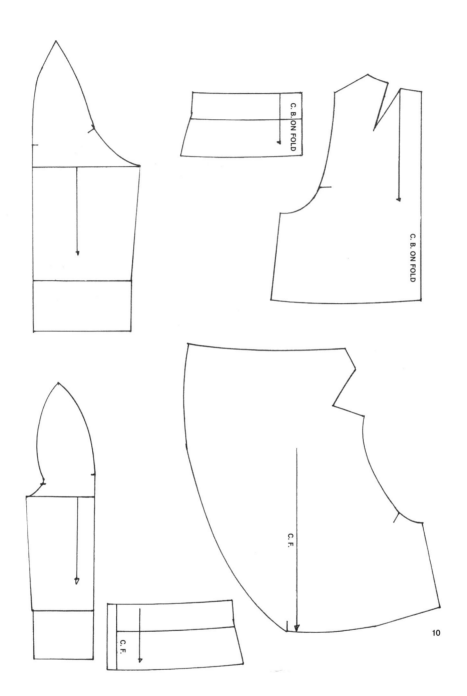

C. B. ON FOLD

C. B. ON FOLD

C. F.

C. F.

10

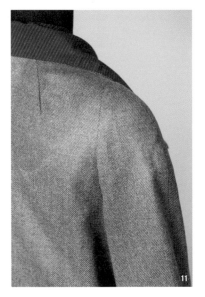

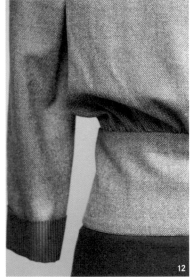

11. The view of the back shows the raglan seam and the slanting dart. This dart position is often chosen for aesthetic reasons. Here, it fulfils its function in a visual way.

12. The gathered expanse of the upper jacket part is caught into the yoke and held. In this way a baggy effect emerges which contrasts with the figure-hugging yoke.

13. The flounce collar is shown to advantage particularly through the use of two different colors. You can let the folds fall freely or fix them with a brooch.

avant et dos. Comme détail supplémentaire, il est possible de dessiner une petite poche au niveau de la ceinture avant.

11. La vue du dos montre la couture raglan et les pinces obliques. La position des pinces sera généralement choisie en fonction de l'esthétique. Elles remplissent donc leur fonction en étant agréables à la vue.

12. L'ampleur de la partie supérieure de la veste s'arrête à la ceinture. Nous obtenons ainsi un effet volumineux qui contraste avec la ceinture qui serre la taille.

13. Le col volanté est particulièrement mis en valeur par la dualité de ses couleurs. Il est possible de laisser les plis retomber librement ou également de les attacher avec une broche.

in die vordere Passe noch ein Täschchen eingezeichnet werden.

11. Die Rückenansicht zeigt die Raglannaht und den schrägen Abnäher. Diese Abnäherposition wird oft aus ästhetischen Gründen gewählt. Hier erfüllt er seine Funktion in einer optisch ansprechenden Art.

12. Die angereihte Weite des Jackenoberteils wird in der Passe gefasst und gehalten. So entsteht ein pludriger Effekt, der zur figurbetonten Passe kontrastiert.

13. Der Volantkragen kommt durch die Zweifarbigkeit besonders zur Geltung. Man kann die Falten frei fallen lassen oder sie mit einer Brosche fixieren.

Figure-hugging jacket with sleeve detail
Veste ajustée avec motif sur les manches
Figurbetonte Jacke mit Ärmeldetail

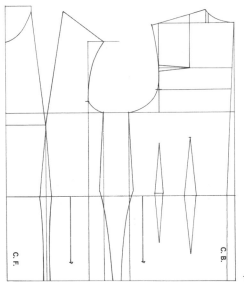

1

1. This figure-hugging jacket demonstrates how you can alter a double-seamed sleeve through an interesting detail in the shoulder area. This change in the cutting is more suited to advanced needlewomen, although – as you can recognize from the pattern – the work compared with the effect achieved is relatively low.

1. Cette veste illustre bien la manière de modifier une manche à couture double avec un motif intéressant sur l'épaulette. Cette modification de la coupe est plutôt destinée aux expérimentés, mais comme il est possible d'apprécier sur le patron, l'effort exigé est minime par rapport au résultat obtenu.

1. Diese körperbetonte Jacke veranschau licht, wie man einen Zweitnahtärm durch ein interessantes Detail im Schu terbereich verändern kann. Diese Schnit veränderung wendet sich eher an Fortge schrittene, obwohl – wie man am Schni erkennen kann – der Aufwand im Vergleic zum erzielten Effekt relativ gering ist.

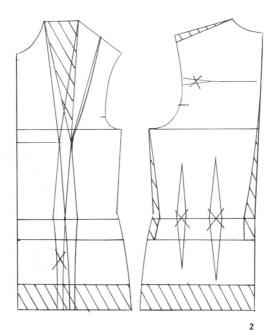

2

2. Starting with the basic pattern for dresses, you draw out the yoke the yoke in the desired width and height. Waist and hiplines always serve as a point of reference. Since leather tears very easily, you should refrain from having darts with this pattern; that means that at the front part a vertical seam – a so-called Princess seam – is inserted so that the darts there can neatly disappear.

The Princess seam at the front is inserted at approximately 3 cm from the side seam so that the pockets worked into the seams are large enough.

At the back you eliminate the shoulder darts by reducing the excess volume in the shoulder seam.

The waist darts are taken out and instead, for the waist, the seam for the centre back as well as the side seam is reduced by about the same amount as the dart.

The darts of the front and back yokes are added and in this way round off the yoke parts.

3. The parts of the front and rear jacket ready for cutting are cut along the grain.

4. The Princess seam is very suitable for having a vertical side slit pocket with

2. À partir du patron de base, tracer les épaulettes suivant la largeur et la hauteur souhaitées. Les lignes de taille et de hanches servent toujours de point de repère. Étant donné que le cuir se rompt facilement, il faut renoncer aux pinces sur ce modèle ; ce qui implique que la partie avant doit comporter une couture principale ou longitudinale, appelée coupe princesse, afin que les pinces soient cachées de manière élégante.

La coupe princesse sur la partie avant est placée à environ 3 cm vers la couture latérale, pour que les poches ouvertes sur les coutures soient suffisamment grandes.

Sur la partie arrière, la pince de l'épaule est supprimée, en réduisant ainsi le volume en trop dans la couture de l'épaule. Les pinces de la taille sont supprimées et, pour compenser, la couture du milieu du dos et les coutures latérales sont réduites de la même quantité de tissu que les pinces afin d'obtenir l'effet ajusté.

Les pinces des épaulettes avant et arrière sont recouvertes et arrondissent les pièces.

3. Les pièces déjà préparées des patrons avant et arrière de la veste sont coupées dans le sens du fil.

2. Vom Kleidergrundschnitt ausgehend, teilt man die Passe in der gewünschten Breite und Höhe ab. Taillen- und Hüftlinie dienen dabei immer der Orientierung. Da Leder sehr leicht ausreißt, sollte man bei diesem Modell auf Abnäher verzichten; das bedeutet, dass im Vorderteil eine Längsnaht – eine sogenannte Prinzessnaht – eingelegt wird, damit die Abnäher in ihr elegant verschwinden können.

Die Prinzessnaht im Vorderteil wird um ca. 3 cm zur Seitennaht hin verlegt, sodass die in die Nähte gearbeiteten Taschen groß genug werden.

Im Rückenteil eliminiert man den Schulterabnäher, indem man das überschüssige Volumen in der Schulternaht reduziert.

Die Taillenabnäher entfallen, stattdessen werden zur Taillierung die Naht der Hinteren Mitte sowie die Seitennähte um den Betrag der Abnäherinhalte verringert.

Die Abnäher der vorderen und hinteren Passe werden zugelegt und runden so die Passenteile ab.

3. Die schnittfertigen Teile des vorderen und hinteren Jackenschnittes werden im Fadenlauf zugeschnitten.

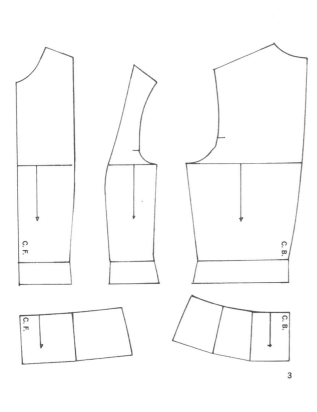

3

4

hidden zip incorporated in it. The pocket pouch reaches up to the centre front and is fixed there.

5. The sleeve is based on the classic double-seamed sleeve, since this goes well with the figure-hugging aesthetics of the jacket because of its narrow fit.
Now the two cut-out parts are prepared. Initially a new dart edge is marked, moving the point of the dart *1 cm* to the right. Since the dart edges should have the same length, the right dart edge is extended in the lower area.
The new point of the dart is linked with a point lying *approx. 4 to 5 cm* above the rear inset marker of the sleeve. Using this line, the new upper arm lines are then drawn in on a convex in each case, at the widest point approximately 0.3 to 0.5 cm, to enable the wearer more freedom of movement. The new upper arm lines in-

4. La coupe princesse est très recommandée pour réaliser une poche insérée verticalement avec fermeture éclair cachée. La doublure de la poche se prolonge jusqu'à le milieu avant, où elle est fixée.

5. La manche, qui s'inspire de la manche classique à couture double, est relativement étroite et s'adapte donc parfaitement à l'esthétique ajustée de la veste.
Réaliser alors les deux pièces de coupe. Une nouvelle pince est dessinée en déplaçant l'extrémité de *1 cm* vers la droite. Puisque les pinces doivent avoir la même longueur, le côté droit est prolongé sur sa partie inférieure.
La nouvelle extrémité de la pince est ensuite reliée à un point situé à *environ 4 à 5 cm* au dessus de l'ajout arrière de la manche. Cette ligne nous permet alors de tracer les nouvelles lignes convexes de l'avant-bras, entre 0,3 et 0,5 cm à l'endroit

4. Die Prinzessnaht eignet sich sehr gut, um darin eine senkrechte Eingriffstasche mit verdecktem Reißverschluss einzuarbeiten. Der Taschenbeutel reicht bis zur Vorderen Mitte und wird dort fixiert.

5. Der Ärmel beruht auf dem klassischen Zweinahtärmel, da dieser durch seinen engeren Sitz gut zur figurbetonten Ästhetik der Jacke passt.
Nun werden die beiden Schnittteile entwickelt. Zunächst wird ein neuer Abnäherschenkel eingezeichnet, indem man die Abnäherspitze *1 cm* nach rechts verlegt. Da die Abnäherschenkel die gleiche Länge aufweisen sollten, wird der rechte Schenkel im unteren Bereich verlängert.
Die neue Abnäherspitze wird nun mit einem Punkt, der *ca. 4 bis 5 cm* über dem hinteren Ärmeleinsatzzeichen liegt, verbunden. Mit Hilfe dieser Linie werden dann die neuen Oberarmlinien jeweils

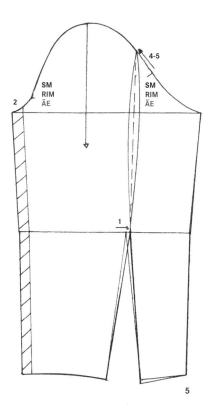

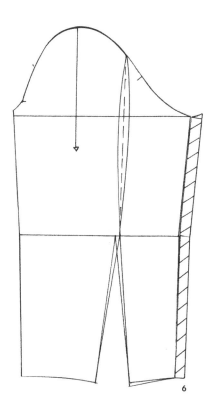

5

6

tersect at the point of the dart; the dart is taken out because of the separation of the parts.

6. The two sleeve parts must be in balance with each other and therefore you lay the lower sleeve seam around *2 cm* to the front, i.e. you detach a 2 cm wide stripe and transfer it onto the right side. It is recommended that you cut into the elbow line to ease the fit.

7. The prepared parts for the sleeves are cut along the grain which runs at right angles to the elbow line. The sleeve has a good fit because of the two seams, and because of the slight bend from the elbow the sleeve fits round the natural line of the arm and in this way enables optimal wearing comfort.

8. The special effect in the shoulder area is achieved by tracing a circular elevation

le plus large, pour faciliter la liberté de mouvement de l'utilisatrice. Les nouvelles lignes de l'avant-bras se séparent à l'extrémité de la pince, la séparation des pièces permet d'éliminer la pince.

6. Les deux pièces de la manche doivent être mises en place de manière équilibrée. La couture inférieure de la manche est pour cela avancée d'environ *2 cm*, c'est-à-dire, qu'une bande de 2 cm de large est retirée puis déplacée à droite. Il est conseillé de couper la ligne du coude pour faciliter la mise en place des pièces.

7. Les pièces de la manche déjà préparées sont coupées dans le sens du fil, qui forme un angle droit avec la ligne du coude. La manche s'ajuste bien grâce aux deux coutures. De plus, le petit pli partant du coude permet à la manche de s'adapter à la forme naturelle du bras et offre une commodité optimale au vêtement.

konvex eingezeichnet, an der breitesten Stelle ca. 0,3 bis 0,5 cm, um dem Träger mehr Bewegungsfreiheit zu ermöglichen. Die neuen Oberarmlinien schneiden sich in der Abnäherspitze; der Abnäher entfällt durch die Trennung der Teile.

6. Die beiden Ärmelteile müssen in einem ausgewogenen Verhältnis zueinander stehen, daher verlegt man die untere Ärmelnaht um *2 cm* nach vorne, d. h. man trennt einen 2 cm breiten Streifen ab und überträgt ihn auf die rechte Seite. Es empfiehlt sich, die Ellenbogenlinie einzuschneiden, um das Anlegen zu erleichtern.

7. Die schnittfertigen Teile des Ärmels werden im Fadenlauf zugeschnitten, der im rechten Winkel zur Ellenbogenlinie verläuft. Der Ärmel erhält durch die beiden Nähte eine gut sitzende Form und durch den leichten Knick ab dem Ellenbogen passt sich der Ärmel darüber hinaus der

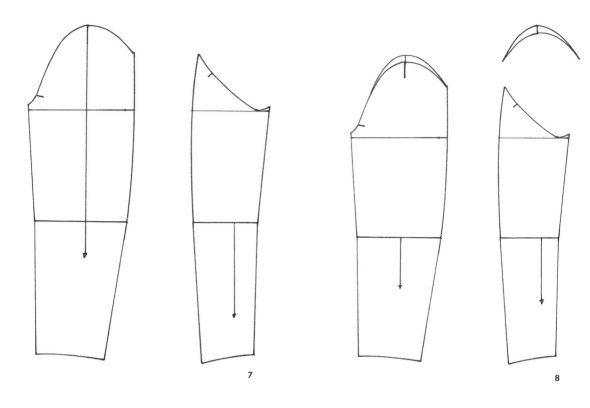

7

8

and copying it as an extra part which is later sewn onto the jacket shoulder. A strong adhesive insert, cardboard or thin plastic material is very suitable for strengthening the leather.

9. A stand-up collar with rounded off corners is added, matching the pattern. It is recommended therefore that you deepen the neckline. In principle the amount, which is enlarged at the point between the neck and the shoulder (shoulder seam), is deepened by a maximum of half at the centre back, as otherwise the collar sticks out or sags at the back. The alteration of the neckline at the centre front on the other hand is optional.

10. Now there follows the cutting-out design for the collar. First of all, you measure the deepened neckline from the front to the centre back, then you cut away half of this value as a length with the end points A and B. Point C corresponds to the mea-

8. L'effet spécial au niveau des épaules s'obtient en dessinant un rehaussement arrondi, une pièce supplémentaire qui est rajoutée par la suite en la cousant sur l'épaule de la veste. Une triplure rigide adhésive, du carton ou du plastique fin peuvent être utilisés afin de renforcer le cuir.

9. Un col élevé aux angles arrondis est ajouté en tant que complément du modèle. Il est pour cela recommandé de faire une ouverture plus profonde pour le col. En général, le segment qui est allongé au point de rencontre entre le col et l'épaule (couture de l'épaule) doit être approfondi au maximum au niveau de la portion moyenne arrière, car sinon, le col se relâche ou retombe à l'arrière. La modification de la coupe doit de préférence se faire sur le milieu avant.

10. La coupe du col doit ensuite être réalisée. Tout d'abord, l'ouverture pour le col plus profond est mesurée de le milieu du

natürlichen Linie des Arms an und ermöglicht so optimalen Tragekomfort.

8. Der besondere Effekt im Schulterbereich lässt sich erzielen, indem man eine Kugelerhöhung anzeichnet und sie als Extrateil abkopiert, das später an die Jackenschulter angenäht wird. Eine starke Klebeeinlage, Pappe oder dünnes Plastikmaterial eignen sich gut zur Verstärkung des Leders.

9. Passend zum Modell wird ein Stehkragen mit abgerundeten Ecken eingefügt. Es empfiehlt sich daher, das Halsloch zu vertiefen. Grundsätzlich sollte der Betrag, der an der Schulterhalsspitze (Schulternaht) vergrößert wird, an der Hinteren Mitte nur maximal zur Hälfte vertieft werden, da sonst der Kragen hinten absteht bzw. durchhängt. Die Veränderung des Ausschnittes zur Vorderen Mitte hingegen ist beliebig.

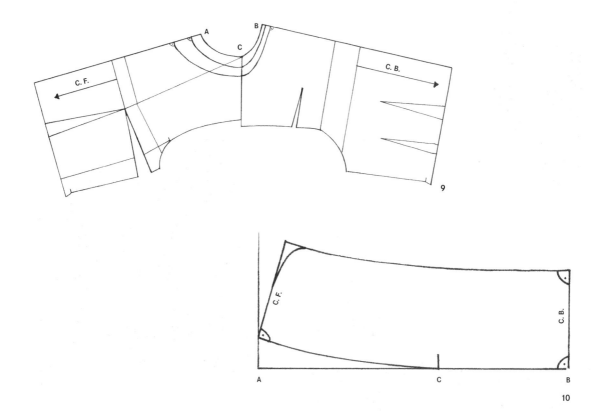

9

10

sured shoulder point where the collar is attached to the shoulder seam.

At point B the collar width is cut away upwards; with this pattern that is 5 cm. This line forms the centre front where the collar will later be cut on the fold.

Point A denotes on the other hand the centre front. Here, you move the end of the collar up for *approx. 1.5 cm to 2 cm* at the angle line meaning that the line of the collar edge is rounded. The collar then fits better into the round collar.

The construction of the rounded corner of the collar begins with an angle line which is drawn from the upper Point A outwards from which again 5 cm of collar width is cut away and where the slightly oval collar neckline is fitted in parallel. The rounded corner of the collar is drawn in.

dos jusqu'à le milieu avant, puis le milieu de cette valeur est reportée entre les points A et B. Le point C correspond au point mesuré de l'épaule, la zone où le col repose sur la couture de l'épaule.

En partant du point B, la largeur de col est déplacée vers le haut ; de 5 cm pour ce modèle. Cette ligne définit le milieu du dos où, par la suite, le col est coupé à part.

Le point A correspond à le milieu avant. Ici, l'extrémité du col est déplacée *de 1,5 cm à 2 cm environ* suivant la ligne angulaire vers le haut, afin que la ligne d'origine du col s'arrondisse. Le col de la veste s'ajuste ainsi mieux à l'ouverture arrondie pratiquée pour le col.

La confection de l'angle arrondi du col s'effectue en traçant une ligne angulaire du point A supérieur, où la largeur du col est de nouveau déplacée de 5 cm et la ligne d'origine du col légèrement ovale est déviée en parallèle. L'angle du col est dessiné arrondi.

10. Nun folgt die Schnittkonstruktion des Kragens. Zuerst misst man das vertiefte Halsloch von der Vorderen zur Hinteren Mitte aus, dann trägt man die Hälfte dieses Wertes als Strecke mit den Endpunkten A und B ab. Der Punkt C entspricht dem gemessenen Schulterpunkt, an dem der Kragen auf der Schulternaht aufsetzt. Im Punkt B wird nach oben hin die Kragenbreite abgetragen; bei diesem Modell sind das 5 cm. Diese Linie bildet die Hintere Mitte, an der später der Kragen im Bruch zugeschnitten wird.

Punkt A bezeichnet demgegenüber die Vordere Mitte. Hier versetzt man das Kragenende um *ca. 1,5 cm bis 2 cm* auf der Winkellinie nach oben, sodass sich die Kragenansatzlinie rundet. Der Kragen lässt sich dadurch besser in das runde Halsloch einpassen.

Die Konstruktion der abgerundeten Kragenecke beginnt mit einer Winkellinie, die vom oberen Punkt A aus gezogen wird, an der erneut 5 cm Kragenbreite abgetragen

11. A nice detail is the leather zipper on the separable 2-way zip which here is sewn in uncovered and ends at the collar line.

12. This jacket stands out because of its figure-hugging fit and its classic style. Stitching leather however needs special previous knowledge. Therefore cloth can be used for this pattern as an alternative, however this should have a certain class, and collars and sleeve detail must be strengthened.

11. La fermeture éclair en cuir dotée d'une fermeture à deux sens détachable constitue un joli détail, avec sa couture visible qui se prolonge jusqu'à la ligne d'origine du col.

12. Cette veste se distingue par son ajustement sur mesure et son style puriste. Il faut néanmoins signaler que le travail avec le cuir exige des connaissances préalables spécifiques. C'est pour cette raison qu'il est possible de réaliser ce modèle avec un autre tissu suffisamment rigide, même s'il est nécessaire de renforcer en plus le col et le motif de la manche.

werden und die leicht ovale Kragenansatzlinie parallel verschoben wird. Die Kragenecke wird gerundet eingezeichnet.

11. Ein schönes Detail ist der Lederzipper am teilbaren 2-Wege-Reißverschluss, der hier unverdeckt eingenäht ist und an der Kragenansatzlinie endet.

12. Diese Jacke sticht hervor durch ihren körperbetonten Sitz und ihren puristischen Stil. Lederverarbeitung bedarf allerdings schon spezieller Vorkenntnisse. Es kann daher für dieses Modell alternativ auch Stoff verwendet werden, allerdings sollte dieser einen gewissen Stand aufweisen, zudem müssen Kragen und Ärmeldetail extra verstärkt werden.

Glossary

An **appliqué** should be stitched to the cut on the fabric.

The **center back (CB)** defines the vertical center line on a pattern for the back piece of a garment.

The vertical center line on the front piece of a pattern, which is traced on a garment, is called the **center front (CF)** and should always be kept exactly in the center.

The **coat flap** is the lower front part of a jacket or coat, between the bottom button or the end of the zipper and the hem.

Crosswise lines are symbols for guidance that are marked on the pattern and should come together when stitching the pieces of cloth together.

A piece that is marked on the pattern but still part of the fabric without stitching is known as a **cut.**

The pieces **cut on the bias** are those parts of the pattern that are cut at an angle of 45 degrees with respect to the selvage, making the garment fuller and helping it to hang more smoothly.

A **dart** is a tuck that is made in a garment and sewn in the form of a triangle (straight dart) or double triangle (shaped dart) to shape the fabric to the contours of the body. It is stitched from the widest part of the dart to the point, and should lie as flat as possible. More details can be found on how to make and move darts on page 10.

The **depth of the pleat** is half this amount. The **pleat distance** is the distance between two pleats.

Ease denotes the additional width that needs to be **eased in.**

Glossaire

La pièce de patron **appliquée** s'assemblera à la **découpe** avec un fil sur le tissu.

Attacher avec des épingles, c'est assembler deux pièces de tissu et les maintenir assemblées avec des épingles à couture.

La **basque** est l'extrémité avant d'un veston, d'une veste ou d'un manteau, entre le bouton situé le plus en bas ou l'arrêt de la fermeture et l'ourlet.

Les **compensations** sont des symboles droits ou arrondis sur des extrémités inégales créées en modifiant le patron.

Le **contenu des plis** est la quantité de tissu qui se trouve à l'intérieur de ceux-ci (non visible de l'extérieur). Outre leur fonction décorative, les plis confèrent plus de confort au vêtement en lui donnant la largeur nécessaire. La **profondeur du pli** est la moitié de cette quantité. La **distance du pli** est la distance entre deux plis.

Les pièces **coupées en biais** sont celles qui se coupent dans le patron avec un angle de 45 degrés par rapport à la lisière du tissu, ce qui améliore la retombée et l'ampleur.

On appelle **découpe** une pièce marquée dans le patron mais assemblée au tissu sans fil.

Égaliser, c'est coudre une extrémité de tissu avec une autre de différente longueur, par exemple, la couture de l'épaule d'un devant avec celle d'un dos, sans que cela fasse des plis. Pour ce faire, il faut étirer l'extrémité courte ou égaliser la longue en les maintenant assemblées.

L'**endroit du tissu** est le côté le plus joli du tissu, celui éventuellement visible dans les échantillons, qui reste à l'intérieur pen-

Glossar

Ein **Abnäher** ist eine Falte im Kleidungsstück, die keil- oder rautenförmig abgenäht wird, um den Stoff dem Körper anzuschmiegen. Sie werden von der Breitseite zur Spitze gesteppt und sollten möglichst flach auslaufen. Weitere Informationen zum Verlegen und Zulegen von Abnähern finden sich auf Seite 10.

Beim **Abstich** handelt es sich um die vordere Kante einer Jacke, eines Sakkos oder Mantels zwischen unterstem Schließknopf bzw. Reißverschlussende und Saum.

Als **angeschnitten** bezeichnet man ein im Schnitt angezeichnetes, im Stoff jedoch ohne Naht verbundenes Teil.

Das **angesetzte** Schnittteil wird im Gegensatz zum dem **angeschnittenen** mit einer Naht im Stoff verbunden.

Das **Ärmeleinsatzzeichen** (ÄE) ist eine Markierung am Ärmelschnitt- und Rumpfteil, das beim Einsetzen der Ärmel die exakte Position bestimmt. Es gibt ein vorderes und hinteres Ärmeleinsatzzeichen sowie ein oberes; letzteres befindet sich an der auf die Schulternaht treffenden, höchsten Stelle des Ärmels.

Die **Ärmelkugel** ist der obere, gerundete Ärmelabschluss, der das Schultergelenk bekleidet.

Als **aufgesetzt** bezeichnet man Taschen oder Applikationen, die auf das Kleidungsstück aufgebracht werden.

Beim **Ausfall** handelt es sich um die Differenz zwischen Hüft- und Taillenumfang.

Ausgleichen ist das gerade oder leicht runde Auszeichnen von sich durch Schnittmodifikation gebildeten, ungleichen Kanten.

asing in means stitching together two ands of cloth of different lengths, such s the shoulder seam of a front piece ath one for a back piece, without any ackering. To do this, the short piece nould be stretched or the long piece ased in, with the fabric being kept to-ather all the time.

acings are pattern pieces that are incor-prated to lend firmness to the garment. ase are normally double thickness or ed for reinforcement.

e fold or fold line is the line along nich the fabric should be folded to join e edges together. The fold line often incides with the straight grain of the bric. Symmetrical pieces of the pat-rn are usually cut "double" so as to tain complete pieces that are exactly e same.

athering means taking in the excess vol-ne in a piece of fabric by making lots of nall creases in the cloth. In long seams, e fabric should be divided into sections that the width of the cloth can be dis-buted evenly.

e grain of the fabric indicates the di-ction of the weave of the cloth, with the reads progressing parallel to the sel-ge. The straight grain of the cloth, which most garments will follow the vertical e of the body, should always be borne mind when cutting out.

e hems are the open seams of the rment, which are finally turned in and mmed or stuck in place. These are ainly the lower edges of the sleeve and e whole garment. The hem is stitched in cordance with the type of cloth.

e intake is the difference between the o circumference and that of the waist.

---

dant la couture et se retrouve à l'extérieur quand le vêtement est fini.

L'**envers du tissu** est le côté du tissu qui doit rester à l'intérieur du vêtement. C'est de ce côté que se dessinent toutes les marques de l'échantillon du patron.

Froncer, c'est reprendre le volume en surplus d'un morceau de tissu en faisant de nombreux petits plis. Dans les grandes largeurs, le tissu doit être divisé en sec-tions afin de répartir la largeur de manière équilibrée.

Un tissu **irisé** est un tissu qui a une image brillante car il est fabriqué avec des fils de différentes couleurs.

La **largeur d'égalisation** est la largeur supplémentaire qui doit être égalisée.

Les **lignes transversales** sont des sym-boles indicatifs marqués sur le patron, qui doivent se rejoindre lorsque les pièces sont cousues.

Les **lisières** sont les extrémités ouvertes, qui se replient finalement vers l'intérieur et se cousent ou se collent. Il s'agit, pour la plupart, des extrémités inférieures du bras et du vêtement complet. Selon le type de tissu, la lisière se coud différem-ment.

La **manche à deux coutures** est une va-riante de manche développée à partir de la **manche à une couture.** Elle se carac-térise par une couture de manche avant et une couture au coude et elle peut mieux s'adapter à la forme du bras.

La **manche avec une couture**, compa-rée à celle avec **deux coutures**, a moins de forme. Il faut donc lui donner avec des plis ou une pince, du coude jusqu'au poignet.

Bruch oder auch **Stoffbruch** ist die Kante, an der ein Stoff gefaltet ist, wenn man die Webkanten aufeinander steckt. Meist ist der Stoffbruch zugleich auch der Faden-lauf. Symmetrische Schnittteile werden oft „Im Bruch" zugeschnitten, um vollkom-men gleichmäßige Teile zu erhalten.

Changierender Stoff erhält durch ver-schiedenfarbige Kett- und Schussfäden ein schillerndes Aussehen.

Beim **Einhalten** geht es darum, zwei un-terschiedlich lange Stoffkanten, etwa die Schulternaht eines Vorder- mit der eines Rückenteils, zusammenzunähen, ohne da-bei Fältchen entstehen zu lassen. Zu die-sem Zweck wird entweder die kürze Kante gedehnt oder die längere eingehalten, in-dem der Stoff zusammengeschoben wird.

Die **Einhalteweite** definiert den Betrag der Mehrweite, die **eingehalten** werden soll.

Einlagen werden verwendet, um Teilen eines Kleidungsstücks, wie beispielswei-se Taschenklappen, Knopfleisten, Kragen usw., die nötige Festigkeit zu verleihen. Einlagen gibt es zum Aufbügeln oder Auf-nähen, als Gewebe, Gewirke oder Vlies.

Der **Einnahtärmel** ist im Vergleich zum **Zweinahtärmel** weniger geformt und wird mittels Falten oder eines Abnähers vom Ellenbogen zum Handgelenk in Form gebracht.

Beim **Einreihen** wird das zusätzliche Volu-men einer Stoffbahn zu vielen kleinen Fält-chen zusammengerafft. Bei längeren Näh-ten sollte der Stoff in Abschnitte unterteilt werden, damit sich die Weite gleichmäßig verteilt.

Der **Fadenlauf** indiziert in einem Gewebe die Richtung der Kettfäden, die parallel zur

Interfacing is used to lend parts of a garment the necessary firmness, such as pocket flaps, buttonholes, the collar, etc. There are interfacings that can be pressed or sewn on, or made of cloth, wool or rib knit fabric.

An **iridescent fabric** is one that has a sheen caused by the different colored threads with which it is woven.

Pattern adjustment lines are straight or round symbols at uneven points created for alterations in the pattern.

Pinning means joining two parts of cloth and holding them together with sewing pins.

The **placket overlap or underlap** is the amount of additional material required in a garment fastened with buttons for the pieces to overlap. The top part, in which the buttonholes will be cut, is known as the placket overlap, with the underlap being the part where the button is sewn on.

The **pleat content** is the amount of fabric taken up inside the pleats (not visible from the outside). Apart from having a decorative function, pleats also make the garment more comfortable, since they give it the right width.

A **raglan sleeve** is a sleeve design in which the seam, with the shoulder incorporated, runs from the cuff to the base of the neck, through the front center piece to the shoulder seam.

The **right side of the cloth** is the best side of the fabric, possibly the one seen in the samples, which remains on the inside during the stitching process and is turned outside when the garment is ready.

La **manche raglan** est une disposition de manche où la couture, l'épaule étant d'une seule pièce, va du poignet à la base du cou, en passant du centre avant vers la couture de l'épaule.

La **marge supérieure** ou **marge inférieure** est la quantité de tissu supplémentaire qui doit exister dans un vêtement boutonné, afin que les pièces se superposent. La partie supérieure du patron, où seront cousus les boutonnières, s'appelle marge supérieure et l'inférieure, ou se coudra le bouton, marge inférieure.

Dans les patrons, nous appelons **milieu avant** (Mav) la ligne verticale centrale de la pièce avant qui se dessine sur un vêtement et qui doit toujours rester exactement au centre.

Dans un patron, le **milieu du dos** (Mdo) définit la ligne verticale centrale de la pièce du dos dans un vêtement.

Une **pince** est un rempli sur un vêtement qui se coud en forme de coin ou de losange, afin d'adapter le tissu à la forme du corps. Elle se coud en diminuant le côté le plus large jusqu'à la partie étroite du coin et doit rester le plus plate possible. Vous trouverez plus d'informations sur la création et le déplacement de pinces sur la page 10.

Piquer, c'est coudre à la machine avec des points droits.

Le **Pli** ou **Pli de tissu** est la ligne où le tissu est plié lorsque l'on souhaite assembler les lisières. Le pli de tissu correspond souvent à la direction du fil. Les pièces de patron symétriques sont généralement coupées dans le tissu plié afin d'obtenir des pièces complètes parfaitement égales.

Webkante verlaufen. Der korrekte Faden lauf – bei den meisten Kleidungsstücke verläuft er senkrecht am Körper – soll beim Zuschnitt unbedingt beachtet we den.

Der **Falteninhalt** ist der Betrag, der sic (von außen unsichtbar) im Inneren ein Falte befindet. Abgesehen von ihrer ve zierenden Funktion sorgen Falten für d Bequemlichkeit eines Kleidungsstücke indem sie die nötige Weite geben. D **Faltentiefe** ist die Hälfte dieses Betrage Der **Faltenabstand** ist die Distanz zw schen zwei Falten.

Die **Hintere Mitte** (HM) definiert in eine Schnitt die senkrechte Mittellinie de Rückenteils bei einem Kleidungsstück.

Mit der **linken Stoffseite** bezeichnet ma die Seite des Stoffes, die bei einem Kle dungsstück innen liegen soll. Auf dies Seite werden auch alle Markierungen de Schnittmusters übertragen.

Passen sind Schnittteile, die am Körp anliegen und so dem Kleidungsstück Ha geben. Sie werden häufig doppelt vera beitet oder mit Einlagen verstärkt.

Querzeichen sind Orientierungshilfe die als Markierungen am Schnitt bei Zusammennähen der Teile aufeinand treffen müssen.

Der **Raglanärmel** ist eine Ärmelanlag bei der die Nähte, die Schulterpartie ei geschlossen, schräg in die Kragennaht b zum Halsansatz, zur Vorderen Mitte od zur Schulternaht verlaufen.

Die **rechte Stoffseite** ist die schöner eventuell mit Musterungen versehene Se te, die bei der Verarbeitung innen, bei fertigen Kleidungsstück aber außen lieg

he **sleeve cap** is the curved upper seam ᵒf the sleeve, which covers the shoulder ₍int.

he **sleeve inset markers (SM)** are ᵊaced on the piece of the pattern for the ₍eeve and bodice, and determine the ex-ₑt position for inserting the sleeve. There ᵃ a mark at the front, the back and the ₍p. The latter is located at the uppermost ₍int of the sleeve, where this joins the ₍oulder.

ᵃ **sleeve with a single seam**, as op-₍sed to **one with two seams,** has less ₍ape and should be fitted using tucks or ₍dart running from the elbow down to the ₍ist.

ᵊe **sleeve with two seams** is a variation ᵒf the sleeve design developed from the **₍eeve with a single seam**. It is charac-₍rized by a seam along the front of the ₍eeve and a seam at the elbow, and can ᵊ more easily adjusted to fit the shape ᵒf the arm.

₍itching means sewing straight stitches ₍sing a sewing machine.

₍atch pockets or appliqués are those that ᵊe **superimposed** or placed on top of the ₍rment.

ᵊe **wrong side of the fabric** is the side ᵒf the cloth that should remain inside the ₍arment. This is the side of the fabric that ₍ould be used to trace all the pattern ₍arkings.

Les **renforts** sont des pièces du patron que l'on met sur le corps afin de donner de la fermeté au vêtement. Ils se placent normalement en double ou se renforcent avec une triplure.

Les **repère d'insertion de manche** (RIM) sont une marque dans la pièce du patron de la manche et du torse qui détermi-nent la position exacte de l'assemblage de la manche au corps. Il y a une mar-que avant, une arrière et une supérieure. Cette dernière se trouve au point le plus haut de la manche, où elle s'assemble avec l'épaule.

Le **retrait** est l'écart entre le tour de han-ches et celui de taille.

Dans un tissu, le **sens du fil** indique l'orientation des fils du tissu, avançant parallèlement vers la lisière. Pendant la coupe, il faut toujours tenir compte du bon sens du fil qui, dans la plupart des vêtements va en sens vertical par rapport au corps.

On appelle **superposées** les poches ou applications posées sur le vêtement.

La **tête de manche** est l'assemblage su-périeur arrondi de la manche, qui couvre l'articulation de l'épaule.

Les **triplures** s'utilisent pour donner le corps nécessaire à des parties d'un vê-tement, comme par exemple les rabats des poches, les boutonnières, le col, etc. Il existe des triplures qui peuvent se re-passer ou se coudre, en tissu, au tricot ou en laine.

Saum/Säume sind offene Kanten, die nach innen eingeschlagen und dann be-festigt werden. Meist handelt es sich dabei um die unteren horizontalen Ärmel- und Kleidungsstückabschlüsse. Je nach Stoffart wird der Saum unterschiedlich genäht.

Beim **schrägen Fadenlauf** werden die Schnittteile im 45-Grad-Winkel zur Bruch-kante hin zugeschnitten und fallen da-durch besonders weich und fließend.

Stecken bezeichnet das Zusammenfügen und -halten von zwei Stoffteilen mit Steck-nadeln.

Steppen meint das Nähen mit der Näh-maschine mit geradem Stich.

Der **Übertritt** bzw. **Untertritt** ist der zu-sätzliche Betrag, der an einem Knopfver-schluss für das Überlappen der Teile dazu gegeben werden muss. Das obere Schnitt-teil, in das die Knopflöcher eingearbeitet werden, nennt man Übertritt, das untere, auf das der Knopf genäht wird, Untertritt.

Mit **Vordere Mitte** (VM) wird auf Schnitt-zeichnungen die senkrechte Mittellinie des Vorderteils bei einem Kleidungsstück bezeichnet, die immer genau in der Kör-permitte liegen muss.

Der **Zweinahtärmel** ist eine Ärmelvariati-on, die aus dem **Einnahtärmel** entwickelt wird. Er zeichnet sich durch eine vordere Ärmelnaht und eine Ellenbogennaht aus und kann somit der Form des Armes bes-ser angepasst werden.

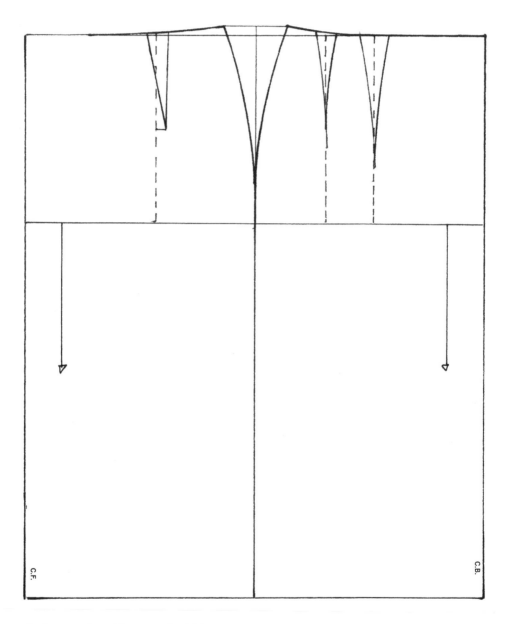

Basic pattern for a skirt on a scale of 1:4
Patron de base d'une jupe échelle 1:4
Rockgrundschnitt im Maßstab 1 : 4

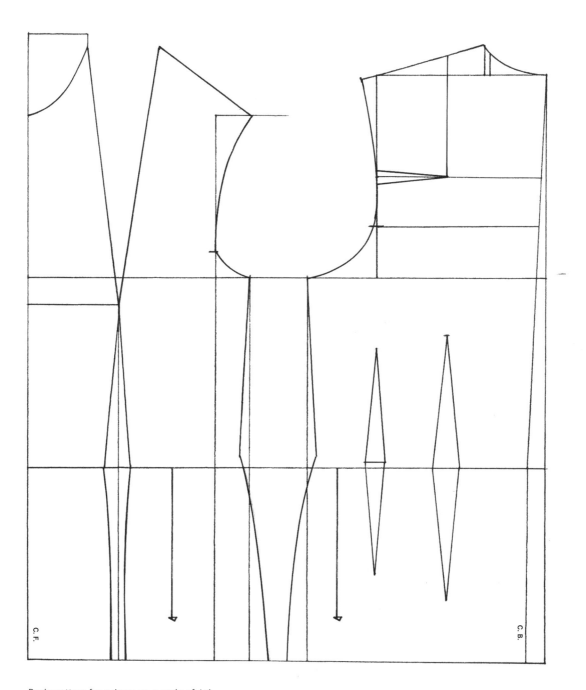

Basic pattern for a dress on a scale of 1:4
Patron de base d'une robe échelle 1:4
Kleidergrundschnitt im Maßstab 1 : 4

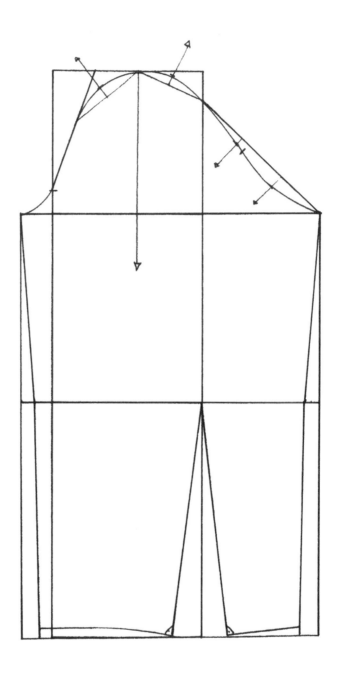

Basic pattern for the sleeve on a scale of 1:4
Patron de base de manche échelle 1:4
Ärmelgrundschnitt im Maßstab 1 : 4